PUBLISHING
& associates

MEN UNDER CONSTRUCTION

Joel Brentlinger

bush
PUBLISHING
& associates

Unless otherwise indicated, all Scripture quotations are taken from the New King James Version of the Bible, copyright © 1979, 1980, 1982, Thomas Nelson, Inc., Publishers.

All Scripture quotations marked KJV are taken from the King James Version of the Bible.

Men Under Construction

ISBN Print: 978-1-944566-81-4

ISBN E-book: 978-1-944566-79-1

Copyright © 2025 by Joel Brentlinger

Bush Publishing & Associates, LLC books may be ordered at BushPublishing.com, Amazon.com, and everywhere online books are sold.

For further information, please contact:
Bush Publishing & Associates
Tulsa, Oklahoma
support@BushPublishing.com
www.bushpublishing.com

Printed in the United States of America.

No portion of this book may be used or reproduced by any means: graphic, electronic, or mechanical, including photocopying, recording, taping, or by any information storage retrieval system, without the written permission of the publisher, except in the case of brief quotations embodied in critical articles and reviews.

DEDICATION

I dedicate this book to you—the reader. I believe that what is written on these pages was inspired by our Heavenly Father, and I pray that I have interpreted His message faithfully.

My deepest gratitude goes to my lovely wife for her unwavering support and encouragement, which carried me through to completion. I also thank my daughter, Michelle Reagan, for tirelessly assisting with the illustrations late into the night, and my dear Yalie, Sophia Brentlinger, whose inspiration helped me press forward with this dream. Every ounce of effort poured into these pages was for one purpose: to bless you.

May the message contained here ignite in the hearts of humankind, resounding across the earth and back again. May countless millions hear the voice of our Father—our Creator—speaking love, redemption, healing, and peace into their lives.

You, dear reader, have been chosen. May you experience true redemption, freedom in Christ, healing in every area of your life, and the power to live as the child of God you truly are. May the Kingdom of God be established in your heart and mind, and may His perfect will be done in your life today.

TABLE OF CONTENTS

Chapter 1 - Who is God? A very good Father! 1

Chapter 2 - Who are you? A Masterpiece! A Son of God. 25

Chapter 3 - Love. A strong floor to stand on. 41

Chapter 4 - Psalm 91. The Prayer of a Warrior. 71

Chapter 5 - The Armor of God! The Shelter of the
Most High God. 93

Chapter 6 - The Prayer of a Father. Pastoring your life well. 115

Chapter 7 - The Final Touches. This is more important
than that. 141

Chapter 8 - Go and Do! The age of the Doers. 173

INTRODUCTION

This is not just another book. It's an invitation—a call to reset your heart, reclaim your identity, and rise into the man God created you to be.

It all started with a simple idea: gather a handful of men, build something with our hands, and build something far greater with our lives. Fourteen men showed up. For eight weeks, we learned about tools, materials, and construction techniques. But what God built in us went far beyond a shed. He built stronger husbands, better dads, and men on fire for Him.

The shed we built was donated to a non-profit in need, but the real project was us. God was shaping men who would lead their homes with courage, faith, and love. And what He did for us, He wants to do for you.

This book is your blueprint for transformation. It's not about fixing you—you're not a project. It's not about pointing out where you're broken—you already know that. This is about revealing the truth of who you are in Christ and opening the door to a life fully alive in God's presence.

Jesus gave everything—His suffering, His death, and His resurrection—to give you a choice. A choice to step out of the ordinary and into the extraordinary. A choice to say yes to healing, redemption, and freedom.

So come in. Step into the Secret Place of God. You are welcome here—just as you are. And once you do, you'll be ready to lead your wife, your children, and your world into the same life-changing love.

There is only one requirement: **Say Yes.**

CHAPTER ONE

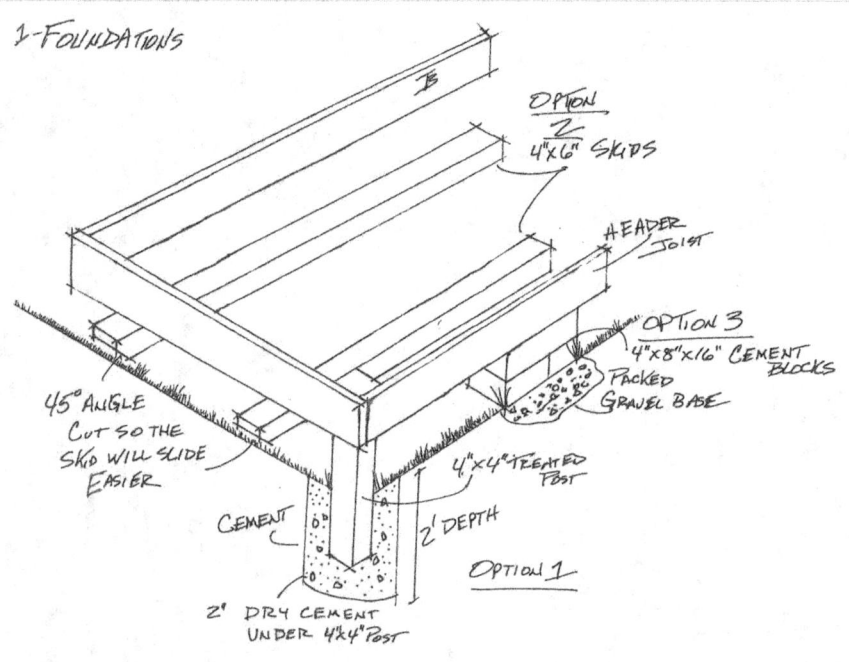

Who is God? A Very Good Father!

The Foundation

> *"In the beginning God created the heavens and the earth."* Genesis 1:1 (NIV)

Our Shed Foundation

There are several different approaches and kinds of foundations we use when building sheds. There are two objectives: 1) soundness and 2) stability. The base structure of the shed must be engineered to be strong enough to support the materials it is built with and the contents it will contain. If it is not, the floor will warp and stretch, causing failure of the walls and roof. If it will be used to store hand-held yard tools, then it could be built lighter than if it will be used to store a riding lawn mower and bags of dirt or cement. Also, the length and width will determine the size and spacing of the lumber used. It's always a good practice to refer to a professional—like an architect—when determining the best design.

The shed can be built remotely, delivered and set at the desired location, or it can be built on site. If it's built on site, I prefer to dig holes and set posts in concrete for the best stability and structural soundness. If your shed will be built off-site and delivered, then rails for ease of movement and concrete blocks for leveling and support are commonly used. 4x4 or 4x6 posts can be used for rails, so we can slide the shed on and off a trailer and eventually into position.

Drawing up or purchasing construction plans is a great way to ensure a good design and help make an accurate materials list. There are plans available online, and some Lowe's and Home Depot stores have design services at the pro desk.

In this first session, we will look over our shed plan, organize some lumber, introduce the tools, learn some simple carpentry techniques, and maybe start on the base structure.

Building a Good Foundation

Foundations are absolutely vital to the success of every good thing. Faulty foundations are the number one tool for our destruction, which the enemy uses against us. A faulty foundation is also the guarantee of certain failures.

In the book of Matthew, Jesus clearly reveals to us how important good foundations are for a successful life. He said:

"Anyone who listens to my teaching and follows it is wise, like a person who builds a house on solid rock." (Matthew 7:24 NLT).

Jesus is telling us that listening to and following His instructions is the foundation for success in life. According to Jesus, not listening and or not following His instructions is foolish because when difficult times come (and they will), our foundation better be strong and stable, or what we "built" on will fail.

In a building, even a small failure of the foundation can cause severe and even catastrophic issues in the rest of the structure. When a structure's foundation is faulty, the damage that the instability will cause could cause the structure to no longer be usable. Therefore, every weakness, fault, and failure begins at the foundation, and every strength and resulting success begins with the foundation.

In our lives, what we believe makes up the foundational structure of our hearts. If what we believe is completely true, then the decisions we make, based on those truths, will stand against all the challenges we face. (Of course, that statement is highly simplified, but we have to start somewhere). For example, If we believe that the sun will come up in the morning, we will plan an activity based on that truth. All of life is this way. If we don't believe the sun will come up in the morning, then we will not plan that activity. (Obviously simplified for explanation.) Look at how King Solomon explains it:

There is more hope for fools than for people who think they are wise. The lazy person claims, "There's a lion on the road! Yes, I'm sure there's a lion out there!" (Proverbs 26:12-13 NLT).

Was there a lion? No. He believed something that was not true, but reacted as if it were and would not leave his house.

This is why the subject of Faith has been taught by Jesus and many others for so many years. While Faith is the **strength** of the foundational structure of our heart, it is not the structure.

"So you see, faith by itself isn't enough. Unless it produces good deeds, it is dead and useless." (James 2:17 NLT).

The structure of our heart consists of many things, but I believe they can be summarized into four divisions: Truth, Trust, Discipline, and Sonship. When our faith in God is strong in the truths of these four basic divisions, we will have a firm foundation to build a successful life upon.

All four of these have a positive, life-giving character and an opposing, negative, deadly character. Are you surprised at that statement? Don't be. Every power has good and bad uses. This is our choice. Electricity is a powerful tool for good, but if you violate the safety rules of electricity, you could get hurt or die. The sun is necessary for life on Earth, but if you don't manage your exposure, it'll kill you. Now I hope you feel better about that statement.

Truth

Jesus told him, "I am the way, the truth, and the life. No one can come to the Father except through me." (John 14:6 NLT).

"No one comes to the Father." This doesn't mean that He is not present, and we have to make an appointment to see Him. This word "comes" is much deeper than that. Our Heavenly Father is everywhere. It references the relationship of a child with his father. When a random person approaches a king, he might get what he wants; he might not. When a child approaches his father, the father asks, "What do you want? What's mine is yours." Jesus did that for us! Jesus, who is Truth, made a way for us to come to The Father just like He comes to The Father. So if we know The Truth—that is, Jesus—then what Truth we know about Jesus will set us free according to what we know and believe.

"And you will know the truth, and the truth will set you free." (John 8:32 NLT).

If you believe, and therefore act on The Truth, at the level with which you believe, it/He will set you free at the level you believed. Jesus cursed a fig tree in Mark 11:12, and it died. His disciples were amazed, but Jesus responded,

"Have faith in God. For assuredly, I say to you, whoever says to this mountain, 'Be removed and be cast into the sea,' and does not doubt in his heart, but believes that those things he says will be done, he will have whatever he says." (Mark 11:22-23 NKJV).

Jesus believed that He had all authority over creation, and it was true! So when His Father gave Him the command to seek out the man at the pool of Bethesda and command him to walk, He did, and the man was healed and walked! Therefore, if we believe a Truth which we have been given, what we are commanded to do will occur if we act according to our faith.

Simplified, if you believe you can move a chair from point A to point B, without a doubt (and probably because you have moved it several times before), all you need to do is go pick it up and move it. It's that simple. But if you don't believe that you can move it, then you won't act, and it will stay right there.

The same is true with our lives. If we believe we can be a better husband and a better dad because we have been told by a reliable source that we can, and if we act on that truth, we will be better. If we don't believe it, then we will never act on it and not only not maintain our current status, but get much worse.

The opposing side is the lie. Truth is very important to know because faith will only work when it is associated with The Truth. For instance, the truth is that Jesus is the Savior of humanity. If you believe in Him and call on His Name, you will be saved. (Romans 10:13) But if you call on the name of some other person, they might be able to help you, but cannot save you from eternal separation from God. If you believe your flight leaves at 3 pm, but it really leaves at 1 pm, you will miss your plane because you believed it was not true. If you believe lies and make decisions based on those lies, the results of your decisions will usually end badly.

Trust in God

"He is my refuge and my fortress: my God, in whom I trust." (Ps. 91:2 KJV).

We should have a good and growing understanding of who God is and who we are. Then we can trust Him even when everything else is crashing down around us. Trust in God only comes when we know who He is, how He does things, and how much He loves us. It requires knowledge. When we know, believe, and then receive His love, we can easily trust in Him. Then Faith can take action.

The opposite of Trust is not trusting. If we don't trust in God, we are always trusting in ourselves or something else. Trust is a choice, and choosing to trust in a lie or something that's not God will end up in disaster.

Discipline

"For God has not given us a spirit of fear and timidity, but of power, love, and self-discipline." (2 Timothy 1:7 KJV).

Paul is telling us here that our Heavenly Father gives us **power** to do what we cannot do without Him, **Love,** which is the motivator of the power and **self-discipline** (or a sound mind in other versions), which is the ability to control our feelings, overcome our weaknesses, and pursue what we think is right despite temptations to abandon it.

It's like using a nail gun or any other tool. When we have it in our hands, we then need motivation to use it, and we need to learn how to use the tool properly, which requires self-discipline. For instance, when we are using a nail gun, it is tempting to use the end of the nail gun as a hammer. But if we do, we will eventually damage the components inside the gun, and it will need to be rebuilt. If we have the self-discipline to learn how to use the tools we have, then we won't misuse them, and they will last much longer.

My dad taught me this when I was little, "Joel, always use a tool for its created use. Don't use a wrench to do the job of a hammer. It takes just as much time to simply go and get the right tool for the job."

Spiritual and emotional issues work the same.

"Remember that people who prophesy are in control of their spirit and can take turns." (1 Corinthians 14:32 NLT).

When we understand why Father created things the way He did, our walk through this life will also be more efficient and effective. This is putting what you believe to use. This is doing what you believe. This is the life of Faith. If you don't do what you believe, then you are simply lying to yourself! And your "Faith" is useless.

"Just as the body is dead without breath, so also faith is dead without good works." (James 2:26 NLT).

So, we need to do more of what we believe. Just like the discipline of reading and researching improves the power of your mind and the discipline of exercising improves the power of your body, doing what you believe improves the power of your spirit. It also increases your confidence. Not in yourself but in The Creator who created you. When you use what you believe and you see it work time after time, your confidence rises and your fear diminishes.

In order to do something well, discipline will always come first. After the discipline has been established, delight comes! Delight is having the confidence to do something well, resulting in the intended results. If you want to delight in the Father, discipline yourself to do what naturally doesn't make any sense—baptize yourself in the Father, Son, and the Holy Spirit. And Baptism requires discipline. We will talk more about Baptism in session 3.

To be baptized means to be immersed in something. If you are baptized in water, you go down into the water and come out of the water. To maintain a balanced life, we must continually be baptized in the Father, Son, and Holy Spirit. This is the Great Commission given to the disciples and to us.

Jesus came and told his disciples, "I have been given all authority in heaven and on earth. Therefore, go and make disciples of all the nations, baptizing them in the name of the Father and the Son and the Holy Spirit." (Matthew 28:18-19 NLT).

We must immerse ourselves in Who Father is. This will require spending quiet, quality time with Him. Just like when we spend quality time with our wife or kids. Sometimes the best quality time we have is when we are simply together and quiet. This requires faith and discipline. Our mind and flesh will tell us that we are wasting our time and not accomplishing anything, but we know that this immersion is one of the three most important things for us to do all day.

I don't know how to explain what happens during my immersion time with my Heavenly Father. Sometimes, nothing is noticeable until later in the day. Sometimes, unexplainable wisdom, peace, answers to impossible questions, and healing in my soul and body. These things happen throughout my day if they don't happen during this time.

This is the Baptism of the Holy Spirit. Not just a single event we call the "Infilling", but a real-life working relationship with the One who is Holy and has my best interest in mind.

The opposite of self-discipline is no discipline. We all know that person who has no self-discipline. They are unpredictable, unorganized, unstable, and not trustworthy. So we should always consider discipline as a very important character trait.

Sonship

There is as much to learn about how to be a son as there is to learn about the Heavenly Father we love. Having a spirit of Sonship is to honor God. To honor God, we honor His creation and His kids as His kids. This is also known as humility or submitting to God's authority, even when we don't understand what He is doing or why.

In the same way, you who are younger must accept the authority of the elders. And all of you, dress yourselves in humility as you relate to one another, for God opposes the proud but gives grace to the humble. (Proverbs 3:34).

So humble yourselves under the mighty power of God, and at the right time he will lift you up in honor. Give all your worries and cares to God, for he cares about you.
(1 Peter 5:5-7 NLT).

When we understand and use these four foundational characteristics, and still experience failures, there is another problem. It's the balance of the four. If we call these characteristic blocks, we could build a platform or a floor on top of them. With one block in each corner, we can place a platform or a floor on top of them.

When we stack bricks on the plywood, everything remains stable. The bricks represent the different aspects of our lives and what we believe. What will happen to our stack of bricks? Nothing, because we chose good things to build our life with and because we have a good foundation to choose from.

This represents the life of a strong believer. It may appear to be boring compared to the miracles of a life filled with loss and recovery. But, it's stable and if maintained, it will become a strong tower, an example of God's grace for all to see! Glory to God!

But if we neglect one of the characteristics, therefore replacing it with the negative side, it's like removing the blocks and replacing them with a balloon. The balloons represent the twisted truths that come from the enemy. They represent the following:

Fear- Fear is actually twisted up faith. Faith in reverse. Faith corrupted...
False
Evidence
Appearing
Real

Fear is the opposite of Faith. For women, it usually causes sadness, emotional imbalance, timidity, and withdrawal. For men, it is the major cause of anger. If we are angry, 99% of the time, we are afraid of something. So when we find ourselves angry, we should ask ourselves what we are afraid of. Fear also leads us to follow after the flesh. Lust, greed, image, addiction, and other self-destructive acts are a result of fear. Being motivated by fear works for a short time and then fails. What are you afraid of? Fear usually begins simply with the thought that we won't have what we need when we need it. So when we see that, we need to kick it out immediately and replace it with the truth! Our Heavenly Father is called Jehovah Jireh, our Provider!

Pride- Pride is the enemy of discipline. You will find a prideful person bragging about how great they are and how they don't need discipline. Pride is also the opposite of Humility. Pride is the violation of the first and second commandments: (Exodus 20) **Have no other gods before Me and do not make idols of them.**

Pride is the act of making yourself a god and taking the glory for things our Heavenly Father has done. Giving God the Glory is giving Him the credit He deserves. The truth is, if it was something good, it was God! Glory is something only God can handle. It's something that belongs to Him alone. Glory will crush us! When we fail to give God all the glory, then we are acting in pride. It works for a very short time and then fails.

Lies- Lies are either slightly or completely twisted truths. The enemy deceived Eve with a twisted truth.

Then the serpent said to the woman, "You will not surely die. For God knows that in the day you eat of it your eyes will be opened, and you will be like God, knowing good and evil." (Genesis 3:4-5 NKJV**).**

It's twisted because the truth is that they were already like God! They just needed to mature, and their Heavenly Father knew when that time should be. Lies may work for a little while to help you get what you want, but it will eventually fail.

Orphan Heart- Just like Sonship is the foundation for all good things, having an orphan heart is the foundation for all the things that are twisted and corrupted in our hearts. When we dishonor people whom we can see, we dishonor God whom we cannot see. This is the root cause of every bad decision. This orphan attitude may get us what we want quicker and easier, but it eventually fails.

The orphan believes he needs to be independent and self-sufficient, so he doesn't ever ask for help. He must **maintain** his image of strength, confidence, and superiority **because** inside, he knows he is really weak. The foundation he is building on is faulty and will obviously fail. Even if some of the things he knows are true, the rest will cause imminent failure.

As we stack the bricks, we can see that it works for a little while. The blocks help, and the balloons do support the bricks to a point. This is an example of our life. We can go to church, go to work, and go home, living at this "surface level" of maturity and knowledge of who God is and who we are. We barely survive until one day the foundation will break. And when it does, usually everything falls, and it's usually disastrous. The degree of disaster depends on how long we have been living like this.

This is why we are here. There are answers and solutions to all of this. It's not easy, but it is simple. You can't just remove lies, pride, fear, or the orphan heart. They can only be replaced with the right things.

As we remove the balloons, which represent the false character copies, we must insert a block.

The orphan in your heart cannot be cast out or simply removed. It must be replaced. And it takes time, discipline, patience, trust in God, and love(respect) for yourself and others. We must replace it with the right things. Fear with faith, pride with humility, lies with truth, and an orphan heart with a heart of Sonship.

The story in the Bible that explains this is in Matthew 12.

When an evil spirit leaves a person, it goes into the desert, seeking rest but finding none. Then it says, "I will return to the person I came from." So it returns and finds its former home empty, swept, and in order. Then the spirit finds seven other spirits more evil than itself, and they all enter the person and live there. And so that person is worse off than before. That will be the experience of this evil generation.

(Matthew 12:43-45 NLT).

The first truth/foundation we will install is about who God is. And like you will hear me say a lot, if you want to know the truth, go back to the beginning. So today we are going to start with removing some of the lies and replacing them with truth from the beginning of our existence.

Who is God?

"In the beginning God created the heavens and the earth." (Genesis 1:1 NKJV).

This word "God" is Elohim in Hebrew or translated The Mighty One in English. But in Hebrew* it has the added meaning, "Father" and "Creator", which makes perfect sense. It is the "Father" who creates. In the beginning, "Father" created all things for us to enjoy.

"Teach those who are rich in this world not to be proud and not to trust in their money, which is so unreliable. Their trust should be in God, who richly gives us all we need for our enjoyment." (1 Timothy 6:17 NLT).

This is who He is and what He does. Father, Creator, and Mighty One are all the same description of God here in this chapter. But when Adam and Eve sinned, they separated themselves from God by taking for themselves something they were warned not to take. Their Creator, Father, told them this for their own good. He needed to mature them spiritually before they could handle Knowledge. Also, He wanted them to choose the food from the Tree of Life first! Father told them to eat of any tree they wanted. That included the Tree of Life! This was His first choice! It's the first recorded time that God left them to decide something without Him being right there. This is our situation and our choice all day long, every day. We have only two choices. Will we choose Life, or will we choose to do things our own way? And they chose to make themselves like God without Him.

When this happened, God changed his name from Father Elohim to Hashem Elohim. Which, according to Wikipedia, is translated as "Lord God". Very different! Now He is Lord, the Ruler and King over His creation. And He is a great king! The best king that we could ever have! But kings have a job and a responsibility! They must make judgments and carry out sentences on those who violate the rules.

So from that day until Jesus, God was known to us as Lord. In the King James version, when you see God's name in the Bible, it's spelled

LORD. All letters capitalized. They used Adoni or Elohim so they would not have to say YHWH. It was too Holy. Can you pronounce it? No. It has no vowels, so it cannot be pronounced. Do you want to know how to say it? Take a big, deep breath. Let it out. You just said God's name! It sounds like a breath! Every time you breathe, you say His name! Over 22,000 times a day, you say His name! Do not use God's name in vain. Remember and highly value every breath! When God created Adam, He said His name over Adam, and Adam came to life! On the day of Pentecost, there was the sound of a mighty rushing wind in Acts 2. The second time God said His name over His people! And what happened? They were filled with His Spirit.

When Jesus came millennia after Adam, he started calling God Father. Because Jesus had that kind of relationship with His Father. He was the Son! And He knew He was the Son! And he called himself the Son in the Gospels! And He lived a life as the Son of God! He was our example of how to live life as a Son of God! This is how we are supposed to live! But Jesus lived His life as a Son because He knew who His Father was. Do we really know who God is? I believe that a lot of us don't choose God and life when we make our decisions because we don't really know who He is. We have this twisted understanding and belief of the character of God. Because of this, many don't want to serve God. I don't blame them.

Maybe you had an abusive father. You will superimpose that image on the definition and character of your Heavenly Father. So we may want to serve him, but we serve him as servants, not as Sons, because we really don't understand who God is. This is a great example of our condition and Father's response.

"On the day you were born, no one cared about you. Your umbilical cord was not cut, and you were never washed, rubbed with salt, and wrapped in cloth. No one had the slightest interest in you; no one pitied you or cared for you. On the day you were born, you were unwanted, dumped in a field, and left to die. "But I came by and saw you there, helplessly kicking about in your own blood. As you lay there, I said, 'Live!' And I helped you to thrive like a plant in the field. You grew up and became a beautiful jewel. Your breasts became full, and your body hair grew, but you were still naked. And when I passed by again, I saw that you were old enough for love. So I wrapped my cloak around you to cover your nakedness and declared my marriage vows. I made a covenant with you, says the Sovereign Lord, and you became mine. "Then I bathed you and washed off your blood, and I rubbed fragrant oils into your skin. I gave you expensive clothing of fine linen and silk, beautifully embroidered, and sandals made of fine goatskin leather. I gave you lovely jewelry, bracelets, beautiful necklaces, a ring for your nose, earrings for your ears, and a lovely crown for your head. And so you were adorned with gold and silver. Your clothes were made of fine linen and costly fabric and were beautifully embroidered. You ate the finest foods—choice flour, honey, and olive oil—and became more beautiful than ever. You looked like a queen, and so you were! Your fame soon spread throughout the world because of your beauty. I dressed you in my splendor and perfected your beauty, says the Sovereign Lord." Ezekiel 16:4-14 NLT).

This was written at a time when the nation of Israel had been captured by Babylon.

Also in Hosea:

"But then I will win her back once again. I will lead her into the desert and speak tenderly to her there. I will return her vineyards to her and transform the Valley of Trouble into a gateway of hope. She will give herself to me there, as she did long ago when she was young, when I freed her from her captivity in Egypt. When that day comes," says the

Lord, "you will call me 'my husband' instead of 'my master.'" Hosea 2:14-16 NLT).

Do you want a Father that you can run to? Someone who will believe in you, be a safe place for you, protect you, teach you, and strengthen you? Good! Ok, let's Google God. Let's look at His track record and see what He has done to prove Himself to us.

The **truth** is always in the Bible! So if we go back to the Bible, we can see who God is and how He does things.

Adam and Eve – To Adam and Eve, He was The Father, Elohim. God gave them very clear and simple instructions about which tree not to eat from. When they sinned, think about how God responded. He didn't come marching through the garden ranting and raving about what they had done. He didn't come in like a storm and destroy everything in His path. He didn't get mad and yell at them. He didn't snap His fingers and destroy them and start over. No! He is a Good Father! This is what a Good Father does. What He created was GOOD! We were created GOOD!

Genesis 3:8 says that as He walked through the garden, He called, "Where are you?" God knew where they were. He was asking them if **they** knew where **they** were. They were in hiding! They had separated themselves from God. This was a call for repentance! Had God separated Himself from them? No. God hadn't done anything! Their Father was calling them to Him! And He still does that today! He still cries through His act of Jesus, submitting Himself to torture, shame, the cross, and hell, "Come to Me! I am your redeemer!" (Isaiah 48:17 KJV)

Haggo'el

In Hebrew, this is translated as REDEEMER! And this is where Father is first called Redeemer:

Then they remembered that God was their rock, and the Most High God their Redeemer.

Psalms 78:35 NKJV

- For Noah, God was his Savior and Deliverer from the evil generation that existed. Father was a Master Builder and a pretty good Zoologist! And don't forget, it was God who created the rainbow and put it in the sky! It was placed there for everyone to remember His promise not to ever flood the earth again with water! God told Noah to COME into the ark. The word "come" tells us that God was already in the ark.
- For Abraham, He was Jehovah Jireh! My God who provides! He made Abraham a dad at 99 years old! Then He provided a ram when Abraham was about to sacrifice his own son. Our Heavenly Father expressed His Faithfulness so clearly to Abraham that he became the Father of our Faith!
- For Joseph, God was the giver and fulfiller of dreams! As Father trained up Joseph in the house of Potiphar and then in prison, He became the Great Administrator! Joseph learned from his Heavenly Father how to govern a nation, from his experience in prison! And He did, famously!
- Then came Moses! For Moses, He was The Great I Am that I Am! Our Heavenly Father sent Moses back to a government that was going to kill him! But he delivered over 3 million slaves from Egypt with Egypt's gold, clothes, and possessions! It was our Father who blew the wind on the waters of the Red Sea, parting the waters which stood up like walls on either side, drying out the sand and mud so they could cross. Then, letting the waters crash in, destroying their enemy! It was Our Father who provided Manna for 3 million people to eat every day for 40 years! He defeated armies, made water come from

a rock twice, caused their shoes not to wear out for 40 years, and brought them into the Promised Land.
- It was our Father who smashed the walls of Jericho for Joshua!
- It was our Heavenly Father who defeated thousands of enemy soldiers for Gideon with only 300 men!
- It was our Father who gave Abraham his faith, Samson his strength, David his courage, Solomon his wisdom, Daniel his loyalty, Moses his humility, Ezekiel his visions, Elijah his power, Peter his fish, Job his long life and family, Nehemiah his wall, John the Baptist his mission, the disciples the Holy Spirit, Paul his Gospel and Jesus…all of us! For Ruth, He was an Honest and Faithful Judge. For Samuel, He was a Great King! For Elijah and Elisha, he was a man of great power and strength. For Jonah, He was the great Redeemer! Our Heavenly Father, of the Prophets, warned the children of Israel of all their twisted ways, and pleaded with them to return to Him again and again and again! He pleaded with them to stop doing what they were doing and repent and change their ways. He warned them to surrender to the Babylonians, in order for their lives to be spared. Again, those who chose Life were spared and given a life in Babylon. Those who refused were killed on the spot. Daniel's Heavenly Father shut the mouths of the lions. He was the 4th Man in the fiery furnace who protected Shadrach, Meshach, and Abednego. For Ezekiel, He was the one who made an army of dry bones grow flesh and come to life!
- For Jesus, His Heavenly Father brought cleansing to the lepers, sight to the blind, hearing to the deaf, new legs, arms, and hands to the lame, food to 4000 and to 5000, life to Lazarus, and healing to the broken-hearted.

- Our Heavenly Father is the one who will lock up the devil for 1000 years just to show those who didn't choose Him that they can live in peace! Then, so they can have a choice, He will release the devil. Many will choose God, and many will not. But this won't last long because quickly Father will grab that devil by the neck and throw him in that lake of fire where he belongs! He is the one who will one day bring heaven to earth forever! No matter what the enemy has convinced you of, our Heavenly Father is Elohim! The Almighty One, the Lion of Judah, the Bright Morning Star, the Savior of the World, the Giver of Life, the Sweet Rose of Sharron, The Lily of the Valley, and the Father of the Faithful!

What has God done for me? I think I have forgotten more than I remember. He's the one who showed up with the money to pay for my daughter's surgery through a series of jobs that I had for six months. One week before the surgery, suddenly everybody paid me, and I had an extra $30,000 in my account after I paid off all my bills.

He was the one who saved me when I thought there was no reason to live as a teenager. He saved me from drowning in a river, from death by gunpoint, car accidents, and several other things. He gave me wisdom that kept me out of trouble. He gave me friends and family who love me. He gave me a gift to touch the hearts of children, and I'm humbled every single time I am around them. He healed my back, my legs, my heart, my eyes, and my stomach. Father, help me to remember these things so I will choose You every time.

What did He do for you? Did He deliver you from pornography? Did He deliver you from drugs or alcohol? Did he deliver you from an abusive situation at home, at school, or at your job? Did your Heavenly Father provide for you when you least expected it? Is your Heavenly Father the one who brought you a beautiful wife, kids who love you even though you're not perfect? Did He give you peace in your heart when there was none? Did He save you from suicide or an immoral life? What did Father do for you? Did he reach down in the middle of your muddy mess and clean you off, stand you up, and put some new clothes on you? And if He did it once, He will do it again! And again! And again! He will never stop. It brings Your Heavenly Father great Joy to see You Blessed and Happy. Receive it now.

Does this help? Yes! So when you get up every morning from this day forward, you are going to say, "My Heavenly Father! I choose You today. All day long, I am going to choose You with every decision I make! Help me choose you!

Why? Because You cleansed me from my sin. You are my redeemer and my righteousness. You bring me back into the right place with You. You are my healer. You are my shepherd. You guide me. You are the one who goes before me and prepares a table for me in the presence of my enemies.

You are My Heavenly Father, and I choose You.

Let our Heavenly Father reveal Himself to you again and again. Seek Him and you will find Him!

*(In the Orthodox Jewish Bible, chapters 1 and 2 use the name Elohim for God. In these chapters, Elohim is the Creator. Up until chapter 3, that is all He has done. According to Karen O'Reilly, at scripturalgrace.com, the name "Elohim" refers to God as the Creator. But in chapter 3, when Adam and Eve sin, God is then referred to as Hashem Elohim. "Hashem" is translated as "The Name" in English.

The Complete Jewish Bible uses God in the first 2 chapters and Adoni in the third chapter in the story where they sin. According to Karen

O'Reilly at scripturealgrace.com, the name Adoni refers to Lord and Master as seen in Psalm 16:2.

Therefore, God was first our Creator, who has an equal description: Father. But after the sin of Man, He became Lord God, or according to the Orthodox Jewish Bible, Hashem Elohim. Using the name "Hashem" demands respect and is used to replace God's unspoken name YHVH. We pronounce it Yahweh or Jehovah. History shows that the priests were very serious about saying this name outside of a very specific time, place, and only the high priest could use it. https://www.betemunah.org/hashem.html Midrash Rabbah's response to this question.

Also, Hosea 2:16 NLT shows how Father's name had changed from Husband to Master, but Father's desire was for it to be changed back to Husband, and He did it through Jesus. And the marriage feast with us as the Bride and Jesus as the Husband in the book of Revelation 19:7.

Put it to Work!

Using the points above, look up the stories in the Bible where God did all these things for us. Don't just try to believe it because I said it was true. Look it up and make what Father did for them, foundational truths for your life.

What does it mean to you? Where is it in the Bible?

1. Adam and Eve- _____

2. Noah _____

3. Abraham _____

4. Joseph _____

5. Joshua _____

6. Gideon _____

What has Father done for you? Your assignment for this week is to make a timeline of significant events that occurred in your life. Events that changed your life or were very important to you. Times when Father showed up in your life. Start with your birth. Continue with times in your life such as when you were Born Again, filled with the Spirit, got married, had kids, etc. Spend some time thinking about all the significant events you can remember. Ask your wife to help you remember these significant events. They can be good ones or bad ones. Bring them with you for the next meeting.

CHAPTER TWO

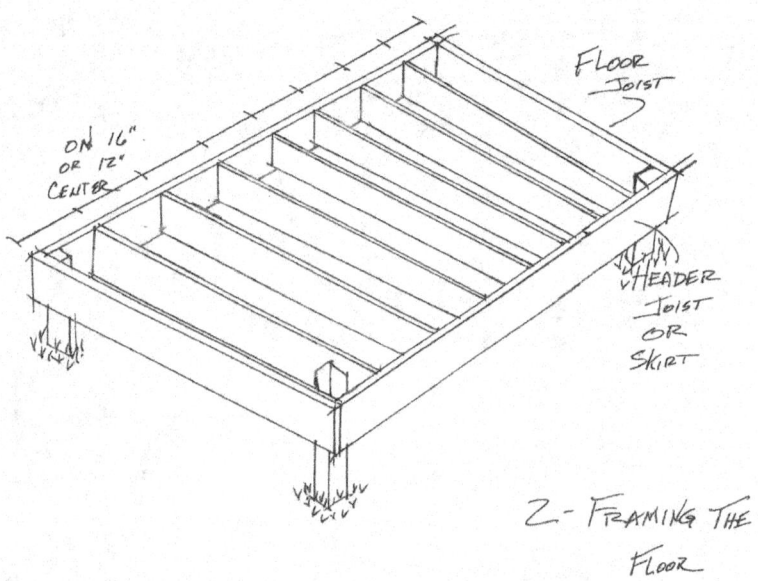

2 - Framing the Floor

Who are you?
A Masterpiece! A Son of God!

I am loved by a God who is good, when I'm not good enough!
Megan Woods

Building the Floor

In this session, we will be building the floor structure for the shed. Each side rail is 2x8 lumber with 2x6 joists on 16" centers. First, we need to look at the plans so we know what we are getting into. We will need:

- Plans
- Tape Measure
- Skill Saw
- Hammer
- Nail Gun
- Nails
- Pencil
- Speed Square

It's good to look over the plans so we know what our overall size should be. With architectural plans, we can actually measure the support beams and joists to see what size they should be. If we have basic design plans—which are not to scale—we just need to know the finished sizes. If our finished size is 8'x12', (The 8' means 8 feet, 8" means 8 inches.) then we will be cutting our long side rails exactly

12'-9" long and the 8' side exactly 8' long. We will cut the inside joists to 7'-9" because we are cutting off 1 ½" from each end, and it will be replaced by the 1 ½" thickness of the 2x8x12' rail. The 2x8 skirts face the front and rear. We don't want the ends of the 12' skirt beams to show.

After cutting the rails and joists, we will first hold up the board on end and look down the board. We are looking for the "crown" on the board. The crown is where the board is bowed up. When you look down the board, you will see it is either bowed up or down. You always want the crown bowed up because when weight is applied, it will fall level. If you put the crown down, when weight is applied, it will bow down even more than it already is. So we turn the crown up before we nail it on.

The next step is to mark the rails for the joist placement. I like to put my rails side by side so I can mark both at the same time. That way, I know they are exactly the same. First, mark your 1 ½" line on either end and mark it with an X. This tells me and others that the end joists go here. Then, from the outside edge, measure and make a mark at 16" for light use and 12" for heavy use. Use a speed square to mark the line all the way across both boards. If we are measuring from left to right, mark an X on the right side of the line. This is where the joist sits. This way we don't get confused and put it on the wrong side. There are several ways to do this. I just chose this one because I thought it was the easiest to explain. Now that we have all our marks, we can assemble.

Set up the rails and end joists on the floor or ground and nail the corners together. I prefer to cut 4x4 posts to fit into the corners. This allows a stronger corner because there is more wood to nail into.

I also prefer to use nails versus screws because screws have a tendency to break when the structure is moving back and forth due to the wind. Nails, on the other hand, will bend and flex.

For the middle joists, we can nail them from the outside of the rails or use joist hangers on the inside. For joist hangers, we can use 1 ⅝" galvanized screws or special ribbed nails designed for joist hangers. Simply line up the joist ends to the lines, and where the X marks the spot.

Now we are ready for the floor next week.

Who are You?

Today, there was a lot of explanation and instruction, and not so much hands-on building. This is the perfect example of the relationship a father has with his son. The foundation of our relationship with our Heavenly Father is built on listening and doing. I attempt to maintain a state of alertness to Father's voice. He can speak through anyone at any time, so if I am listening for Him, I will usually hear Him. At least I'm poised to hear Him. If I am caught up in myself, then I am turning a deaf ear to Him because I am not poised to hear Him. My loss. When I am not in the place of teaching, I am usually listening to others so that I can learn something new. This is the attitude of a Son, which we should attempt to maintain.

God always works through lines of authority first. This is why He speaks especially through people who are older than us or have some sort of authority over us. This is why humility and submission to authority are so important.

Some of us had dads that were loving, spiritual, and functioning awesomely, but some of us had dads that were either not present or abusive, and all of us had those dads in between. The more absent or abusive dads gave us a poor image of who our Heavenly Father is and how He prefers to do things. The really good dads gave us a pretty good idea of who God is, but still were not perfect in all they did. Why is this?

After studying dads in the Bible, I found it was hard to find a man whose legacy was great children. I can find lots of great men of God, but not many great dads. Think about it. Adam? Nope. Noah? Probably not. Moses? We never hear about his kids. But he did mentor Joshua, who eventually took his place of leadership. Oh! King David! Nope. Absalom tried to take the throne from him, and King Solomon turned out pretty good and then crashed in his latter years. And, Solomon's kids were hardly mentioned except for the one who became king after Solomon, and he was pretty bad.

There are only 2 dads that had a legacy that I have found: Abraham and Elijah. Abraham is still looked up to today as the Father of our Faith and the Father of pretty much the whole Middle East. Even the Muslims love Abraham today. He had a legacy of successful children, 4 generations down to Ephriam and Manasseh. Elijah took on Elisha as his apprentice, and he turned out pretty good. I believe Elijah was a great dad because he is mentioned in prophecy.

"Look, I am sending you the prophet Elijah before the great and dreadful day of the Lord arrives. His preaching will turn the hearts of fathers to their children, and the hearts of children to their fathers. Otherwise, I will come and strike the land with a curse." (Malachi 4:5-6 NLT)

An angel said this to Zachariah, John the Baptist's dad:

"And he will turn many Israelites to the Lord their God. He will be a man with the spirit and power of Elijah. He will prepare the people for the coming of the Lord. He will turn the hearts of the fathers to their children, and he will cause those who are rebellious to accept the wisdom of the godly." (Luke 1:16-17 NLT).

I believe scripture refers to John the Baptist as the one making the way for the Messiah of the generation of Sons and daughters to the world. Jesus was the Master Son! And He continues to be the Master Son for generation after generation.

At the time of my writing this, I was returning from a trip to Italy. Italy was the flourishing capital of the Roman Empire. Absolutely amazing works of architecture, many of which still stand today. The Roman Empire was massive, had a horrible reputation for worshiping every god whose worshipers they conquered, and they were probably the greatest persecutors of the new Christian faith of the time. But it was also the time Jesus came to the earth! Israel wanted a Savior, and we all got one! Our fathers made their way to Rome and evangelized. Eventually, Rome got evangelized and saved, and today there are over 900 churches in Rome, mostly from many centuries ago. (Facts found at Wikipedia.com).

Our Heavenly Father conquered Rome with the Gospel of Jesus, our Savior. On my trip, I saw the remnants—still standing—of probably the greatest revivals this world has ever seen. Why else would the people build such mammoth buildings? There was only one colosseum in Rome and one in Verona left standing, but hundreds of churches, bell towers, baptismals, and great works of art which are known around the world! That's how our Father works! He loves to create legacies.

Is this stirring up a question in your heart? Maybe, "How do I become a great dad and create a great legacy?" The answer is:

Become a great son!

There will be many "fathers" in our lives and none of them will be perfect. The reason is so we learn to seek and find our Heavenly Father on our own. Even though our fathers are not perfect, our Heavenly Father will still use them to speak to us, often. This is why we must learn to honor our fathers.

"Honor your father and mother." This is the first commandment with a promise: If you honor your father and mother, 'things will go well for you, and you will have a long life on the earth." (Ephesians 6:2-3 NLT).

The dynamic between Heavenly Father, father, and son is absolutely amazing. As a father, we hear from our Heavenly Father so we can give our kids direction and encouragement. If we don't hear from our Heavenly Father, our kids miss out and so do we. And of course, our goal is to teach our kids how to hear from God for themselves, so one day they will hear God for their kids. This is how we were designed to work together! But if the communication between any of the three breaks down, the whole situation becomes much more difficult. Our Heavenly Father is perfect in all His ways, and He always has our best interest in mind.

Knowing who God is is the first and most important part of our foundation. But knowing who we are—a Son of God—and being the best Son we can be, is just as important. If you don't know who God is, you can't believe in Him, trust Him, or depend on Him to help you.

But if you don't know who you are, you won't ever ask for help, even if you do believe He is willing and able to help you!

A few years ago, I heard this story from the great evangelist, Reinhard Bonnke:

There was a farmer who lived in the mountains. One day, while riding into the mountains to round up his cattle, he saw an eagle's nest that had fallen to the ground in a storm. He thought for sure the mama eagle had died in the storm because the little baby eagle, all alone in the wild, would surely be eaten by some coyote or bobcat. So he picked up the baby eagle, put him in his pocket, gathered up his cattle, and went home.

When he got home, he put the baby eagle with the chickens, hoping the mama hen, who had chicks, would take him in and care for him. Sure enough, she did! Like the other chicks, the mama hen taught that little eagle how to hunt for food. They hopped around and ate worms, grasshoppers, and all kinds of little bugs. Day after day, the mama hen cared for the little eagle. It didn't take long for the chicks to grow out their feathers, but the little eagle just got bigger and more fluffy. The other chicks made fun of the eagle because he kept growing taller and skinnier and still had his fluffy chick feathers.

After a few months, the eagle finally grew out his feathers, but now he was very tall and much more skinny than the now fat, round chickens. They laughed at him, saying "What is wrong with you? You are brown, and real chickens are white. You are tall, skinny, and weird looking! We are short, fat, and beautiful! And you are always looking up into the sky. Chickens don't look into the sky. They look at the ground. That's probably why you're so skinny. You don't eat enough bugs!" Even the mama hen would scold the little eagle saying, "Stop looking up to the sky! We don't fly! You need to find food to eat! Scratch and dig up some bugs! Act like a chicken! You're embarrassing me!"

So the little eagle tried to be a good chicken, but he just couldn't fit in. Then one day, they heard a screech far off. Mama hen called to all her chicks to run for cover! And they all ran into the brush and under the trees! But the little Eagle was curious. "That sound is familiar," he thought. Mama hen was calling and calling to him, "You're going to get eaten by the eagle! Hide!" Then suddenly, the mama eagle saw her long-lost son! She cried a loud screech and dove closer to the ground. The little eagle screeched back. It was his first time! He had always tried to cluck like a chicken, but couldn't. The mama eagle screeched and screeched as she flew in a circle above her son. Then the little eagle saw his mama's wings and thought, "That looks familiar."

So for the first time, he spread his wings! He flapped a couple of times, and his feet came off the ground! He thought, "Chickens can't fly!" The mama hen and the other chickens cried for him, telling him that if he doesn't hide, he will for sure get eaten! But the mamma eagle screeched, "Fly, my son! You're an eagle like me! Fly!!" So the little eagle's heart changed. He spread his wings and flapped as hard as he could, then he took a big jump! Off into the air he went! Immediately he screeched, "Bye-bye, chickens! I'm an eagle!" And he flew up, up, up high into the sky! He was never a chicken! He was an eagle!

Who are you? Are you a chicken or an eagle? Have you been told by the world that you are a stupid, weak, helpless, hopeless chicken?

That is what we are talking about today. We need to know who we are! In the beginning, you were formed by the very hands of God! (Genesis 2:7) God said, "Let there be light!" (Genesis 1:3) And light was. He spoke, and the land formed. He spoke, and the plants, animals, sun, moon, and stars appeared! God spoke all of creation into existence. But when He created us, He got down on His hands and knees, gathered some dirt and some water, and with His hands, He formed the first man! Then, He took a big breath, breathed over the first man, and the man came alive!

So, you and I were created in the very image of God. Think about it.

We were made just like Him!

Let that sink in for a minute. I have been criticized so much for that statement. Why? Because most people don't want to take on the responsibility of being made like God. Or they don't want to be like God; they just want to please Him so they don't go to hell. Please don't be "that dad" or worse, "that son". Just stop all your thoughts and narrow them down to one idea: We are His Masterpiece.

"Salvation is not a reward for the good things we have done, so none of us can boast about it. For we are God's masterpiece. He has created us anew in Christ Jesus, so we can do the good things he planned for us long ago." (Ephesians 2:9-10 NLT)

We are a masterpiece in God's mind. Wow! I may like a certain work of art and think it's just wonderful. But my opinion really doesn't matter to anyone because I am no one special. But the Creator of All Things thinks YOU ARE A MASTERPIECE! That's significant! **He** said that we were made in **His** image **and** likeness. He said we were **good!**

"Then the Lord God formed the man from the dust of the ground. He breathed the breath of life into the man's nostrils, and the man became a living person."
(Genesis 2:7 NLT).

"So God created human beings in his own image. In the image of God he created them; male and female he created them."
(Genesis 1:27 NLT).

"Then God looked over all he had made, and he saw that it was very good! And evening passed and morning came, marking the sixth day."
(Genesis 1:31 NLT).

So just take a minute and meditate on these scriptures. Read them over and over. Consider the TRUTH about them.

We were made to handle His power and have His Spirit live within us! When God created us, He said we were **very good** in Genesis 1:30.

"How you made me is amazing and wonderful. I praise you for that. What you have done is wonderful. I know that very well." (Psalm 139:14 NIV).

In Isaiah 43:1-4 God said, "I called you by name and you are mine!"

In Psalm 100:1-5 He called us the sheep of His pasture.

Psalm 17:6-9 says He hides us in the shadows of His wings!

In Psalm 139:1-18 we are His masterpiece, woven intricately by His own hands. He saw us and loved us before we were even born!

In Psalm 18:16-19 He delights in us!

In Hosea 1:10, God calls us His Children and His people.

In Zechariah 2:10-13, God calls us His Special possession.

Deuteronomy 28:1-14 says that we are Blessed! If we follow after our Father, we will be blessed when we go in and blessed when we go out! Everything we put our hands to will be Blessed

Then at the right time, Father came as Jesus who willingly gave His life for us. That's when everything changed. Paul said this in the book of Ephesians.

All praise to God, the Father of our Lord Jesus Christ, who has blessed us with every spiritual blessing in the heavenly realms because we are united with Christ. Even before he made the world, God loved us and chose us in Christ to be holy and without fault in his eyes. God decided in advance to adopt us into his own family by bringing us to himself through Jesus Christ. This is what he wanted to do, and it gave him great pleasure. (Ephesians 1:3-5 NLT).

For he raised us from the dead along with Christ and seated us with him in the heavenly realms because we are united with Christ Jesus. For **we are God's masterpiece.** He has created us anew in Christ Jesus, so we can do the good things he planned for us long ago. So now you Gentiles are no longer strangers and foreigners. You are

citizens along with all of God's holy people. You are **members of God's family**. Together, **we are His house**, built on the foundation of the apostles and the prophets. And the cornerstone is Christ Jesus Himself. We are carefully joined together in Him, becoming **a holy temple for the Lord.** (Ephesians 2:6, 10, 19-21 NLT).

We became **heirs of a promise**! United with Christ, seated with Him in heavenly places, God's Holy People, the very Temple of God, filled with the Holy Spirit, Blessed coming in and Blessed going out.

We have right standing with God, peace with God, Joy in the Holy Spirit, and authority in Jesus.

Have you been believing that you are someone that you are not?

Let me tell you who you are! You are a Son of God! You have access to the Faith of Abraham!

The Humility of Moses.

The leadership of Joshua.

The strength of Samson.

The courage of David.

The wisdom of Solomon.

The power of Elijah and Elisha.

The legacy of Daniel.

The tenacity of Job.

But as a Son of God and joint Heir with Jesus, through Him we can forgive sins, restore the broken-hearted, be fathers to sons and daughters, heal the sick, make blind eyes see, deaf ears hear, lame people walk, and raise the dead.

"For we are God's masterpiece. He has created us anew in Christ Jesus, so we can do the good things he planned for us long ago." (Ephesians 2:10 NLT).

I am born of God, and the evil one does not touch me (1 John 5:18 NLT).

I am an ambassador for Christ (2 Corinthians 5:20 NLT).

I am part of a chosen generation, a royal priesthood, a holy nation, a purchased people (1 Peter 2:9 NIV).

My body is a temple of the Holy Spirit; I belong to Him (1 Corinthians 6:19).

I am the light of the world (Matthew 5:14).

Close your eyes. Nobody can read your mind. Nobody knows what you have done or what you haven't done. Silently confess where you are. Confess the current state of your heart. Your faults, your true desires, your thoughts, your deepest longings to your Heavenly Father.

Don't worry. Your Heavenly Father can take it ALL. He TOOK it all on the cross! Go ahead! Unload on Him! Dump it all out. Everything you can right now. If you can't unload everything, it's ok. We all have a lot to deal with. It's like peeling an onion. We have layers and layers to go through, and it's healthier to deal with one or two things at a time than talk about a lot of things and not really do anything about any of it.

Even now, your success is not measured by how much you can confess, but by whether you will. You may not be willing to give up some things right now. You may be so addicted to whatever it is that is killing you, that you would rather rip your hand from your arm than give up your "thing". If you feel like this, just try to be willing, to be willing. It's a start in the right direction, and our Heavenly Father knows the struggle you are facing.

Now, here comes the healing! Father will not let you wallow in your pain forever if you receive Him. Wrap your arms around Him and receive His love for you! Submit all of your heart that you can.

"Even before he made the world, God loved us and chose us in Christ to be holy and without fault in his eyes. God decided in advance to adopt us into his own family by bringing us to himself through Jesus Christ. This is what he wanted to do, and it gave him great pleasure." (Ephesians 1:4-5 NLT).

Pray with me. Father, help me see myself as You see me. Help me to serve you, always choosing You with every choice I make. Make me the Son that you want me to be. Renew my mind, cleanse my heart, and fill me with Your Spirit today.

Homework:

What did you learn today about building a shed?

_____

_____

How did you see yourself before today?

_____

_____

How do you see yourself now?

_____

_____

What did you learn today about how you were created?

_____

_____

What did you learn today about how you can be a better Son?

_____

_____

What did you learn today about how you can be a better dad?

_____

_____

CHAPTER THREE

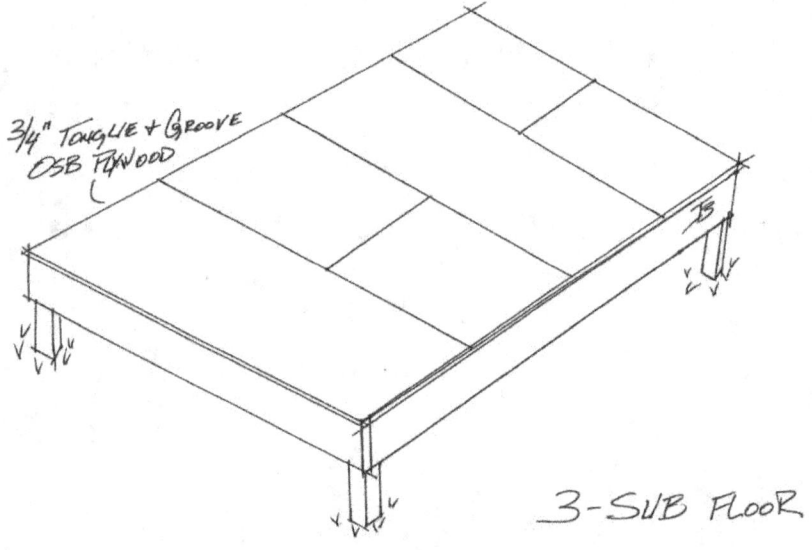

Love
A Solid Floor to Stand On!

"Love never fails." (1 Corinthians 13:8).

Let's Build it!

This time we will build and nail down the sub-floor onto the frame and maybe frame up some walls. We will still need the same tools plus some glue.

Today, we will be using ¾" T&G (tongue and groove) OSB. OSB stands for Oriented Strand Board. Typically called the subfloor. But since we won't be putting anything on top of it, it will serve as our floor. The great thing about plywood and OSB is that they come in nice, rectangular sheets with squared corners. OSB is also called chipboard. They take large wood shavings, spray them with glue, and press them together with heat. Then, when cured, they cut the frayed edges to make 4'x8' sheets. This is similar to how plywood is made, but plywood is made from large sheets of thinly shaved logs. That's why you will see patterns in plywood repeat. Then they lay the sheets with the grains crossed, spray glue between the sheets, and cure with heat and pressure. I'm not an engineer, but I think the plywood is stronger than OSB. Although Plywood, today, is more expensive. In homes, on suspended floors, 1 ⅛" T&G is used. A waterproof 1 ⅛" OSB. is available. It is great to use in wet conditions, such as bathrooms. Water makes normal wood swell and separate, but not the waterproof kind.

The tongue and groove system is used so the sheets are linked together, so the seams stay at the same height, and there is strength at the seams between the floor joists. I like to glue the seams to seal them from insects in our shed application. It's not necessary with a shed, but in houses, we glue the subfloor to the floor joists (which we will do) to keep the screws and nails from loosening and eventually causing that creaking sound you hear in older homes. What you hear is the sound of the nails sliding in and out of the wood. The glue stops that.

If you measure sheets of T&G OSB, you will notice that the sheets are not exactly 48"x96". This is because there is a space ¼" designed into the sheets for thermal expansion. If the sheets were the exact 4x8, when they got hot in the summer, being fitted together exactly, they would buckle. So there is space for expansion built into the size. When we lay the sheets, we will leave ¼" space between the sheets for this reason. You can make any repair in a wood subfloor with this knowledge.

After laying the subfloor, we will frame up what walls we have time for. This is the exciting part! I always get this amazing feeling of accomplishment when things start going vertical. Just like the floor framing, we can calculate the length of the 2x4s and build the wall on top of the floor for accuracy.

I have worked with children from 4 to 18 for over 25 years. I deeply enjoy having the privilege of being an example of Jesus to children. I had one girl, in Kids Church years ago, who I got to know when she was in first grade. She was a pretty little girl. Sweet, kind, helpful in the classroom, smart, and just a really good kid. She began to call me grandpa after a few short months. I enjoyed sitting on the floor with the 20 kids in the class, telling stories from the Bible. This little one would often snuggle up next to me so she could follow along when I read. This always made me a little uncomfortable, but I felt there was a good reason for her attachment to me. I noticed that her grandma always brought her to church, and I never met her parents.

Two years passed, and one day I asked the group a question about their parents. It was not specific to anyone. I was about to make a point using the information I was expecting to get. When I looked over at this little girl, tears were rolling down her face. I asked if she was ok. She sniffled and strongly said, "Yes." Later, I caught up with her grandma to tell her what happened and asked if she was ok at home. Then I began to hear her terrifying story.

Her dad left when she was little. Her mom was on drugs. She grew up in neglect, mostly alone, so her grandma tried to help and take care of her. (This all happened before she started coming to our church.) Then one day, this girl, 5 years old at the time, and her mom were driving somewhere when the mom got mad at her. She stopped at a gas station, opened the door, kicked her out, and drove off. Neither the girl's mom nor dad wanted her. She was truly orphaned. How sad! Who would not want this beautiful little girl for a daughter!? So I was determined to give her the opportunity to experience my "Father's love" and maybe some healing could begin.

The next Sunday, I taught a lesson on the orphans of the Bible and how God was such a good Father to them, and how He raised them up to do great things in the world. Men like Joseph, Moses, Esther, Ruth, and Samuel. Some of these had parents but were disconnected from them, and some didn't have parents at all.

But there is a Father for the orphan, and He is humble and gentle in heart toward His kids.

"Sing to God, sing praises to His name; Extol Him who rides on the clouds, by His name Yah, and rejoice before Him. A father of the fatherless, a defender of widows, is God in His holy habitation." (Psalms 68:4-5 NKJV).

Without Him, you don't have a floor to stand on.

Without our Heavenly Father, there is no safe place, no security, no care, no peace, and no love. But if you choose Him, my Heavenly Father will be your Heavenly Father and will heal your heart, love you, and bring peace back into your life.

Today, I want to introduce you to this vital concept of the heart of an orphan versus the heart of a Son. First, we talked about Father. Last session, we talked about how you were created a Son of God. Today, we are going to talk about what it looks like **to be** a Son.

Jesus said this right before He ascended into heaven:

"Therefore, go and make disciples of all nations, baptizing them in the name of the Father and of the Son and of the Holy Spirit."

(Matthew 28:19 NIV).

Baptism is a spiritual event of immersing in something. We can be immersed in water. That's water baptism. A testimony of our faith. So first, we must immerse ourselves in Father. This is what we did in Session 1.

Second, we must immerse ourselves in the Word of God. Jesus is the Word made flesh.

"In the beginning, the Word already existed. The Word was with God, and the Word was God." (John 1:1).

Your Bible contains the very Words of God, the Creator of all things. Our words may carry value or not, but Father's words always carry much value. They paint a picture of who He is, how He does things, and how much He loves us! His Words are not sent out without doing what they say (Isaiah 55:11). His words are true (Ps 119:160). His words are life for us (John 6:63). Genesis 1 says that with His Words, everything we know was created. So we must immerse ourselves in His Word so we can become more like Him.

"By His divine power, God has given us everything we need for living a godly life. We have received all of this by coming to know him, the one who called us to himself by means of his marvelous glory and excellence. And because of his glory and excellence, he has given us great and precious promises. These are the promises that enable you to share his divine nature and escape the world's corruption caused by human desires." (2 Peter 1:3-4 NLT).

Third, we must immerse ourselves in the Holy Spirit. Not just be filled with the Holy Spirit but do the works the Spirit does. It's the Spirit of God "working" **within** us and **through** us, doing the things we do all day long. If we do not immerse ourselves in the Holy Spirit, we become unbalanced. This is why, when we have prayed and fasted and seen no results, or memorized scripture and read the Bible all the way through, but still saw no results. We were unbalanced. We need to be immersed in Father, Son, and Holy Spirit. Jesus said,

"I can do nothing on my own. I judge as God tells me. ...I carry out the will of the one who sent me, not my own will." (John 5:30 NLT).

Jesus did nothing without the Holy Spirit guiding Him and empowering Him because He immersed Himself in the Holy Spirit.

People ask me all the time, "How do you hear from God so clearly?" My answer: I talk with Him all day long. He talks with me. I read

His words and therefore I am familiar with how He thinks. But most importantly, I do my best to **do** everything He tells me. Doing what He said is the proof that I heard from Him.

This is BEING a Son of God! But when we decide to do things on our own without the Holy Spirit, we orphan ourselves from Him. Let's look at that.

A good starting point is to identify the opposite of being a Son—being an orphan. Are you an orphan in the physical sense? Somehow, you were separated from your parents? You know what it is like to not have a home, a safe place, someone who loves you and cares for your needs. I believe this process, which we are going through together, will offer you a path that will result in the healing of your heart. Or maybe you had a dysfunctional family that left you orphaned in many other ways. Or maybe you had a good, safe, loving family, but something is still missing, and you feel unloved and unfulfilled, but confusingly enough, without reason. Even if we were raised in a really good, Christian home, we all deal with orphan issues.

Believe what I am about to say. Your Heavenly Father is poised and ready to be all those things you are missing. He never leaves you, and He deeply desires for you to know He is present with you all the time. But for you to be aware of His presence, you must invite Him into your "space" and be determined to make yourself aware of Him. If we don't invite Him into our space, a downward spiraling series of events begins.

And here is where the problem lies—kicking God out of our space. This is a progression that leads to the place where you may now be in one or more areas of your life.

12 Warning Signs

1) Offense
2) A Wounded Heart
3) Basic Trust is Lost
4) Gentle guidance is replaced by rules.
5) We harden our hearts against the pain and become defensive.
6) In defense of our pain, we begin to become self-reliant, closing ourselves off from others.
7) We need to be in control either passively or actively.
8) Relationships suddenly become superficial.
9) We become overwhelmed by our own needs and weaknesses and can't find the answers, which leads to depression and panic attacks.
10) We have no safe place to rest, and a replacement for love must be found.
11) Addictions take root.
12) What you were controlling now controls you! Spiritual oppression.

We will dive deep into this later, but with this 12-step progression, we can see how we got into the trouble we are in, or at what stage we are at in our issue.

This is why we need a good, solid, flat surface to build on. It is very difficult to build a level wall on a non-level floor. I've done it and it's not fun. But in residential buildings, we do it all the time. Why? Because they usually pour the concrete for homes sloppily. They don't take the time to level the forms, so the walls have to be shimmed from the bottom because they must be level at the top, or the roof will be crooked and everyone will see it.

As for the quality, the **level of foundation of our heart,** we learned in the first session that these deep foundational characteristics cannot simply be removed. They MUST be replaced. That's why behavior modification is not the solution to our problems.

Everything in life is this way. Every addiction and destructive behavior replaced a good, healthy behavior, so the bad must be replaced by the original good again. Even a semi-healthy behavior—for a time—is ok if it helps us press through to the better choices.

A good example is drug addiction. I have a friend who was on some medication, which he later discovered was causing more problems than it was solving. But he couldn't just stop taking it, or his body would go into a shock of some kind. (I am not a doctor or a professional in this area. I'm just telling you what happened.) So he had to begin reducing the amount until he was no longer taking the medication. This decision was made by a knowledgeable doctor and was a healthy and wise choice. Some bad behaviors need to be cut off at a dead stop. Some need to be cut back at a determined pace until they no longer control us. I also say this because sometimes when we decide to cut off a bad behavior and replace it with good behavior, we slip and do it again. If this happens, receive your forgiveness and start again. Don't let your enemy convince you that if you mess up, you're done. This is a fight! And sometimes we get hit when we are in a fight. Now, don't use this as an excuse to enjoy your old behavior and ask for forgiveness later. AND, I am talking about less destructive issues like eating too much or drinking too much caffeine. I am NOT talking about abusing yourself or others! Those behaviors need to come to a complete stop. For those things, seek accountability and professional help to do this.

Destructive behaviors are fueled by twisted fantasies of pleasure without pain.

Real pleasure, that our Heavenly Father created us to enjoy, will require respect, honor, and discipline. This is a pain we are willing to endure because the outcome is worth it. So, when we feel a desire to lust or have sexual thoughts about someone—not our wife—(pleasure without discipline), we are really thirsty for time with our Heavenly Father. This is warning number 10–replacing love with something fake. No, Father allowed this void in our heart so we would seek Him to fill it. It's a battle at first, but when (not if) you get those thoughts, shift your attention from that to your Heavenly Father and His Word, acknowledge His presence with you, and learn to use the Helmet of Salvation (Which we will talk about later). When we do that, their influence over us will be reduced to almost nothing.

It's this private conversation with Father that we actually thirst for.

Our enemy knows this truth and will jump in quickly to offer a lie and a counterfeit affection in place of the true desire we have.

When we first experience pain, we will make one of two choices: be offended and run or turn to Our Heavenly Father for comfort and healing. The experience of discipline at an early age is actually a precious time of deep bonding with your child. I believe I only had to spank my kids for a few short years early in their lives because I learned this process from a spiritual father of mine.

When you need to spank a two or three-year-old, you first tell them not to do something. They must understand that you don't want them to do what they are doing. You may need to tell them many times before they understand that what they are doing is wrong. Then you watch for the rebellious attitude. That's when they need a little spanking. Little ones are rarely rebellious. They are simply experimenting, curious, adventurous, and wanting to learn new things and have new experiences. So gentle guidance is all that is needed. They learn what "no" means quickly. This is how I taught my kids not to touch something hot, like the stove top.

One day, when I was cooking, Michelle came up to see what I was doing. She was just tall enough to reach up and just old enough to be curious and want to do what Dad was doing. So I pulled up a little stool for her to stand on up close to the stove. Then I showed her the burner, the flame, and the pot of boiling water. I told her to be careful because it was hot. Then I gently took her hand with mine and brought it close to the burner, carefully, just to let her feel the heat. Not enough to burn her. I'll never forget how she looked at me, pulled her hand back, and I said, "Hot". Michelle never burned her hand on the stove. If I warned her that something was hot, she backed away.

Other things were not so easy, such as teaching her to share her toys with other kids at about two years old. I don't remember an exact experience, but it would go something like this: I would tell her not to do something or, for instance, to share with her sister. She would get mad and refuse to share. I would calmly encourage her to share and show her how fun it is to share. If she resisted that, she might get mad and throw the toy, hitting her sister with it and causing her to cry. Then I would quickly but gently take hold of her, turn her around so we are looking eye to eye, and say, "I said no." Then I would spin her around and swat her bottom–not hard. Believe me, it doesn't take much. It really doesn't hurt her bottom. It hurts her heart more. Not her physical heart, her emotional heart. Then she would start to cry, and I would turn her back around and hug her and hold her until she stopped crying and was comforted. This incident might happen at 2 or 3 years of age. After that experience, I usually would only have to warn her and never have to spank her for the same thing twice. I needed to show her the consequences of her actions because I love her. Never, ever spank a child out of anger.

Love protects and disciplines, but is primarily the healer and the comforter.

I am disciplining her in order to avoid future and greater problems. I am building safe boundaries for her to make choices within. This gives a child a tremendous amount of security and knowing that they are loved. Now, at the time of this writing, since my kids are older, I see the tremendous amount of confidence they have concerning right and wrong, which has made them very stable adults. Thank You Father for giving me that instruction when they were little.

When we discipline in this way, we create pain <u>with</u> healing, and the child will begin to run to us when they encounter pain instead of from us.

If we don't discipline in this way, we form the foundations of orphan thinking in their heart. When children are hurt by someone, they will pull away from them emotionally or run to them for comfort. But what if we disciplined wrong? What if we did it out of anger, or if the harm we caused our child was accidental? In all these cases, we failed to comfort our child after the pain was inflicted. When this happened to us, this is when, as children, we felt hurt and rejected and chose the lonely path of the orphan. But when presented with the Gospel of God's love for us, Jesus' sacrifice, and desire to fill the empty place in our hearts, children choose Jesus easily.

I see it constantly with kids 3 to 5 years old. They don't have but this one sin they are struggling with. They chose to distance themselves from an authority emotionally. Usually, it's their parents, but it could be someone else they looked up to. And now their heart is orphaned from God, and inside they are sad and alone and don't know what to do about it. When they hear about Jesus, they know He is the answer, and they easily accept Him. We all choose this path at one time in life. That is why we need a Savior.

Many times and under many circumstances, we choose the orphan path. We don't go to our Father with the issue and seek Him for comfort and answers. We cut ourselves off from God, hide the pain, and try to modify our behavior so no one knows. This is when the enemy quickly shows up with a fake replacement for the love we so desperately need, and the downward spiral of painful events begins.

We see this first complete example in Genesis with the story of Cain and Abel. Able offered a good sacrifice for his sins, and Cain did not. Where is Adam? He is not around. I am guessing that Adam was already such an orphan that he wouldn't repent and receive healing. So he was not there to help when Cain was going through this painful event. So God stepped in and tried to help by reminding Cain that if he just did it right, everything would be ok. Father caught him early—the perfect time to correct is at the time when we are making that decision—But Cain refused. Instead of humbling himself and receiving the warning as an instruction that would save him pain, he chose to be hurt and then refused to go to Him for comfort. And, "sin was crouched at the door." (Genesis 4:7), and he accepted the alternate solution for his pain—killing Abel. This is how an orphan thinks: get rid of the problem person, and we won't have that problem anymore. This was not defense; it was murder.

But our good example was Jesus!

"Jesus grew in wisdom and in stature and in <u>favor</u> with God and all the people."
(Luke 2:52 NLT).

Jesus had favor with God **and** with people. Jesus was a Master of Sonship. He never allowed His heart to be orphaned from God or people.

There is a reason for the need to be a healthy Son, like Jesus. We were made by Love, for Love. We were designed **to love** in powerful, amazing ways! We were designed **to be loved** in powerful and amazing ways, too! But if we don't follow the correct path of the actions of love and being loved, we will find something or someone to replace the void that only **Real Love** fills. The issue is the definition of love that has been created in our hearts from the experiences we have had and the resulting choices we have made.

Because of differing life events, we all have different definitions of love, like we had different definitions of "father" and "son". So today, we are going to define Love.

This is what real Love looks like.
1 Corinthians 13:4-8 NIV
Love is patient,
love is kind.
It does not envy,
it does not boast,
it is not proud.
It does not dishonor others,
it is not self-seeking,
it is not easily angered,
it keeps no record of wrongs.
Love does not delight in evil
but rejoices with the truth.
It always protects,
always trusts,
always hopes,

always perseveres.
Love never fails…

Many see love as a sappy, soft, fragile, second-rate, unpredictable emotion. Love is actually the greatest, most powerful, most consistent force there is. For orphans, love is reduced to a tool of bribery to control others. It is a show performed to get approval from someone. Love for an orphan is nothing more than a "low-level emotion" or a rule that must be followed to get a desired result.

How do you see 1 Corinthians 13? Do you see it as a set of rules that must be followed? If you do, you are thinking like an orphan. Do you see it as a standard you must live up to? This is orphan thinking. Is it painful for you to consider asking your Heavenly Father to teach you how to be patient? This is orphan thinking. When you understand the unmatched power of Love empowered Patience, as a Son who knows that his Father will always come through for him, you will eagerly ask your Heavenly Father for Patience.

A Son recognizes 1 Corinthians 13 as the character of his Heavenly Father and how he is treated by his Heavenly Father. He, in turn, desires to act like his Father, and he has the capacity to do it! As we begin to live in the power of Father's Love, Love in all these forms will begin to radiate from us.

This is how the early Christians won the hearts of the Roman Empire.

This is how we will win the hearts of the world!

Love is Patient

I would say that Love is primarily and foremostly Patient. Patience for a Son is applying Faith and strong Trust in His Father with expectation for His desire to manifest! Patience is a very powerful tool that we should learn to master. It reveals gentleness, which governs a mighty strength residing within us. It makes us stronger than our enemy. It creates strength in our character that others see, and as a result, they feel more confident in our decisions. Real Patience is powerful! It is Love in motion!

Patience is leaning heavily on your Heavenly Father, waiting faithfully until He shows up. And He will, when we are Patient!

When everyone else is freaking out, you can be patient. You will be surprised how quickly things happen when we engage Patience and Faith compared to when we don't.

Patience for an orphan is nothing more than the act of painfully putting up with some naïve idiot until he can get what he wants.

They have little concept of Patience because they can't trust anyone. They will always be in a hurry at everyone's expense, not willing to wait for the outcome. If they don't get what they want, when they want it, they usually throw a fit and sadly never receive what they actually desire. They will settle for less every time.

Sons will wait in Faith, believing God for His Best. Being empowered with Patience always pays off. Receive the Patient Love of God.

"The servants who are ready and waiting for His return will be rewarded. I tell you the truth, He Himself will seat them, put on an apron, and serve them as they sit and eat!" (Luke 12:37 NLT).

Love is Kind

Kindness is a defining characteristic of our Heavenly Father. When His Love shows up in our lives as kindness, it almost always acts like a force. The force of Kindness, which comes from our heart, will wreck an angry, broken heart. We can be Kind to someone who has hurt us because Father has been Kind to us! Usually, the Force of Kindness comes out when an orphan has hurt us. Instead of reacting and lashing out to hurt them back, we turn to our Heavenly Father and seek His Love. At the perfect time, His Kindness will come flowing up from within our hearts. When it does, we'll have the strength to Love, be Patient, and then be Kind to the one who was rude to us. **That's when their life gets changed!** They will see Love instead of the punishment they are used to and expecting. The Force of Kindness will wreck their heart and change their life. They will see a Love that can only come from Our Loving, Heavenly Father. They will be amazed and want to know how we can do that.

The orphan does not know how to be kind. He thinks kindness is fake because he doesn't feel like he deserves that kind of love. The orphan only knows revenge, and they will resort to it quickly. The orphan's "love battery" is empty, so he cannot love back. He is powerless to change the heart of someone else and is therefore always on the defensive. Orphans will find fault in everything and everyone but themselves. Instead of appreciating the beauty of a flower, the most an orphan can do is pick it instead of stepping on it. They cannot see the good in others, so they cannot access any strength on the inside to be kind.

If you find yourself in a situation where you just don't have the strength to be kind, you know your "love battery" is at least low and probably dead. So stop and turn your heart to your Heavenly Father for a 5-minute recharge. Like when your drill battery is dead, Stop, Hook Up to the Source, and "Charge Up" (SHUSCU) on Love from your Heavenly Father. Read your Bible (even if you don't understand it), talk with Him, be grateful for anything good around you, worship Him with some good music, and sit and be quiet with Him. Kindness is a huge witness and sets us apart as Christians—Little Christs! It's what Jesus did on the cross when He said,

"Father, forgive them because they don't know what they are doing." (Luke 23:34).

This horrible feeling of anger and revenge must be replaced by Father's Love. There is no better replacement. Then you can be Kind to others and watch what Father does through your kindness.

Love is not proud or envious

For your sake and because Your Heavenly Father is Jehovah Jireh, Your Provider, you have no reason to be envious or have pride! Sons have no reason to be envious, jealous, or proud. Orphans are always jealous of others and proud of themselves. They never think they have enough and so always want what someone else has. If they do get a little something, they probably stole it or cheated to get it, and what they get is never enough. They will always brag about what they got, but it will still never be enough. This is pride.

Am I proud of my kids? Sure. This is actually the best definition in our culture today. But I'm not really "proud" in the negative sense. When I talk about my kids, I don't talk about what **I** have done that made them so successful, like **I** was the only one involved. I'll talk about how **they** worked so hard and suffered the pains of being highly responsible, and how **God** moved in our lives. I will tell you about certain things I did, but only as an example for you to follow. Love is not envious because **He is** the Source of all things! Love is not jealous because **He has** everything! Love is not proud because **He is** the Mighty One! And Sons have no reason to be envious or jealous or proud because they know who their Father is and they know they have full access to Him all the time! As Sons of the King of Kings, we must understand and know that we are Sons of Royalty. A Prince of the King of Kings has no reason to be envious because all he needs to do is ask, and he has.

"For everyone who asks, receives. Everyone who seeks, finds. And to everyone who knocks, the door will be opened." (Matthew 7:8 NLT).

A Prince has no reason to be proud because he knows that he did nothing to earn what he has. Everything is given to him. He knows that Father is his source for everything he has! When you feel envious or jealous or proud, remind yourself who your Father is and that you are His Son. You have everything you need, and He fulfills the desires of Your Heart.

Love doesn't dishonor or cut someone else down

Our Heavenly Father knows something about honor!

"Whoever serves me must follow me; and where I am, my servant also will be. My Father will honor the one who serves me." (John 12:26 NIV).

Love always honors others above itself. Have you ever heard God ask you a question? Why would He do that when He already knows everything?

Because He Honors you as His Son!

Like you respect your kids—their likes and dislikes—Father respects and honors you. There are numerous scriptures concerning honor.

"For husbands, this means love your wives, just as Christ loved the church. He gave up his life for her. (Ephesians 5:25 NLT).

"So again I say, each man must love his wife as he loves himself, and the wife must respect her husband."(Ephesians 5:33 NLT).

Children, obey your parents because you belong to the Lord, for this is the right thing to do. "Honor your father and mother." This is the first commandment with a promise: If you honor your father and mother, "things will go well for you, and you will have a long life on the earth." (Ephesians 6:1-3 NLT).

Love will rise out of your heart (when you believe it) to honor those around you. It's most difficult when you need to honor someone who has authority over you, and either you have a "better" idea or they have poor judgment. There have been many books written about this subject, but to summarize, with honor comes promotion. And promotion is the only way to get out "in front" enough to be an "Influencer".

No honor, no inheritance.
No inheritance, no influence.
No influence, no promotion.

Dishonor is a key sign of an orphan heart. Orphans will always cut someone else down to prove that they are better. They desperately strive to keep the image of themselves up, most always at someone else's expense. Orphans will not honor those who do not benefit them. They always have to be right.

A Son, on the other hand, will build others up at his own expense because he knows his Heavenly Father will be building him up soon. Sons don't depend on others to tell them, "Good job!" or "Thank you!" Their Heavenly Father does that. Orphans get mad and feel rejected if they don't get the recognition they think they deserve. Sons learn to look only to their Heavenly Father for approval.

The feeling of approval is absolutely vital to our existence.

The lack of this feeling can cause depression and despair. It's a trap door leading to a deep, dark abyss of failure. The only way out is to seek approval from Your Heavenly Father. This is why religion is so deadly. Religion says that we must "do this or that" to be approved;

this is a lie! Father sent His Son so we could **choose** His approval! He may not agree with what choices we make, but He will still defend us as His own Kid because He chose us first. He may discipline you with His Word, but you will always be His Son. You can honor others because Love Honors others.

Love is not self-seeking

Sons know where their provision comes from because they know their Father is Faithful! Orphans always seek to supply their own needs because they believe that no one will ever help them. Orphans get depressed because they are consumed by themselves. If an orphan is telling someone about a problem they are having, you will hear them saying "I" and "me" and "my" a lot. That is why they are depressed! They are looking to themselves for the answers and can't find them. And they won't! They don't have the answers. If they did, they wouldn't be in the mess they are in! Love does not seek to have its own way or its own desires fulfilled at the expense of others. Love is selfless. Love thinks of others first at its expense. How? Because Father loved us first, filled us with His Love, and now it overflows!

"For God so loved the WORLD that He GAVE His only Son that whoever believes in Him shall be saved!" (John 3:16).

Love does not seek its own but looks to seek out what others are in need of first. Sons do not need to suck the life out of everyone around them because they are a Fountain of Life themselves, empowered by Love.

Love is not easily angered

"But you, Lord, are a compassionate and gracious God, slow to anger, abounding in love and faithfulness." (Psalms 86:15 NIV).

Love will defend those He loves. I am pretty easy to get along with until you threaten my wife or kids. Then, you'd better stand back because I have no fear. Sons have no reason to get angry because they have no fear! Their Father always gives them everything they need, so they have nothing to fear! Sons have enough confidence in their Heavenly Father that they can support others and help them when they are afraid. Orphans live in fear. Fear of everything is their primary motivation. An orphan will act like a rough, tough, confident bully only to prove that he is not afraid, when inside he is scared to death, unpredictable, and unstable. Real strength does not come from having control but from a gentle, patient, and dependable heart full of love.

Love doesn't keep a record of wrongs

"Praise the Lord, my soul, and forget not all his benefits— who forgives all your sins and heals all your diseases, who redeems your life from the pit and crowns you with love and compassion, For as high as the heavens are above the earth, so great is his love for those who fear him; as far as the east is from the west, so far has he removed our transgressions from us." (Psalms 103:2-4, 11-12 NIV).

Walking in forgiveness requires continuously recharging our Love Battery. Sons can forgive because they are reminded that they have been forgiven. In their humility, they are seeking their Father for help because they know they can't do anything productive on their own. They can forgive because they remember how they were forgiven and know they are being forgiven daily for whatever wrongs they are doing.

Orphans can't forgive. Orphans will act like they forgive only to keep up a "spiritual image". They will complain and talk badly about what happened to everyone except the one they need to forgive. A Son will always forgive because he knows that unforgiveness is the seed of bitterness. A Son with a heart full of love, and being filled with love from His Father, will not want to risk cutting himself off from that flow of Love being poured into him. He would rather have a wrong done to him than do wrong to others. An orphan only thinks about his pain and what benefits him. Love is the Gift of forgiveness. It's the "Gift that keeps on Giving!"

Love does not delight in evil but rejoices with the truth

"Blessed is the one who does not walk in step with the wicked or stand in the way that sinners take or sit in the company of mockers, but whose delight is in the law of the Lord, and who meditates on his law day and night." (Psalms 1:1-2 NIV).

Sons rejoice when truth wins out because they are huge advocates of Truth and success! Orphans rejoice when someone gets taken advantage of or gets hurt. They laugh when they lie to get something, and someone is dumb enough to believe them.

An orphan will always feel satisfaction and delight over someone else's loss. When others crash, an orphan feels like, "It's about time someone feels like I do". Orphans feel delight when others are cut down because they believe they will finally stand taller than everyone else. He will celebrate when someone fails. Orphans cannot feel the pain of others. They only feel their own pain, and it plagues them constantly. They have no compassion because they don't really know what love is.

Sons know and feel the pain of others. They remember what it was like to hurt when they had a loss, and they are ready to express comfort from the abundance of comfort they are receiving from their Father. A Son will also eagerly rejoice when others win! Even if he was competing for the same thing. This is the love of God that constantly fills the heart of a Son who positions himself to humbly receive from his loving Father.

I've seen this in my daughter's life. When she was in high school, she participated in fierce public speaking competitions. And even though she spent hours and hours for months preparing for this one event, when she lost, she enthusiastically congratulated the winner. Everyone was amazed at her exceptional sportsmanship and her love for others. Love rejoices with the truth.

Love always protects, always believes, always hopes, always perseveres

May the God of hope fill you with all joy and peace as you trust in him, so that you may overflow with hope by the power of the Holy Spirit. Romans 15:13 NIV

Sons will always stand up and protect the weak—their wives and kids, especially. Sons will choose to believe instead of doubt. They will choose to believe in you first and wait to be proved wrong at their own expense simply because Love Believes. Love can also see when someone has faith and can sense a lie, because lies come from fear, and fear is the opposite of faith. You can't use your faith in something that is not completely true.

Because Love believes, it also Hopes! A Son Trusts in his Father and so has Hope for the best outcome in every situation. And watch how that works in your life. I have seen the difference in the life of someone who lives believing for the best all the time and someone who is always negative and critical of every outcome.

Orphans cannot hope. For them, hope is nothing more than a wish. For sons, hope is the thing that ties them securely to their Heavenly

Father, whom they know will never let them down. Even when things don't go the way they thought, Sons have put everything in their Father's hands, and they know everything will turn out for their good.

"And we know that God causes everything to work together for the good of those who love God and are called according to his purpose for them." (Romans 8:28 NLT).

Orphans are always disappointed in every outcome because things never turn out the way they thought they would. This is perseverance. A Son will stand in the rain of a storm and refuse to complain because he knows that His Heavenly Father has His hand on things. Even in death, his Father can take the worst and make it the best. Love protects, believes, hopes, and never quits because Love is the most powerful force there is. It was out of His Love for us that He endured the cross and won victory over Hell, to redeem us. This was Father's biggest move of faith and love.

And finally, Love never fails!

"No one will be able to stand against you as long as you live. For I will be with you as I was with Moses. I will not fail you or abandon you. This is my command—be strong and courageous! Do not be afraid or discouraged. For the Lord your God is with you wherever you go." (Joshua 1:5, 9 NLT).

My favorite part! Love is the strongest force there is! Love is not some weak, soft, fragile, fickle, girly, unstable emotion! Love is the definition of "Manly"

Only Our Heavenly Father can define real Love for us. In the same way, the best person to define real Love for his family is DAD!

Love is not conquerable. Love always wins! Jesus' love for us is what led Him to the cross, down to the depths of hell, out again, and all the way to the right hand of God. He did nothing wrong but took our punishment upon Himself so we wouldn't have to! No one has ever done that for anyone! Love is The Way of the Son! And Love can empower you to BE the Son of God that is in you! The Love of the Father—that can be in you if you choose—can empower you to do the things Jesus did and the greater things that He promised.

So the question remains. Who are you? You know who you were created to be. Now, who will you choose to be? Which Father will you choose? Whose Son will you choose to be?

Today I have given you the choice between life and death, between blessings and curses. Now I call on heaven and earth to witness the choice you make. Oh, that you would choose life, so that you and your descendants might live!

"You can make this choice by loving the Lord your God, obeying him, and committing yourself firmly to him. This is the key to your life. And if you love and obey the Lord, you will live long in the land the Lord swore to give your ancestors Abraham, Isaac, and Jacob." (Deuteronomy 30:19-20 NLT).

So what is Love?
1 Corinthians 13:4-8 NIV
Love is patient,
love is kind.
It does not envy,
it does not boast,
it is not proud.
It does not dishonor others,

it is not self-seeking,
it is not easily angered,
it keeps no record of wrongs.
Love does not delight in evil, but
rejoices with the truth.
It always protects,
always trusts,
always hopes,
always perseveres.
Love never fails…

Questions:

What aspect of Love encourages you the most?

_____

_____

What aspect of Love do you excel in?

_____

_____

What aspect of Love do you need to grow the most in?

_____

_____

How full is your Love Battery?

_____

_____

Do you remember when you chose to be offended and started thinking down the path of the orphan?

_____

_____

Homework:

Meditate on the condition of your heart in all the areas of your life. We can be solid or partial Sons of God in some areas and solid or partial orphans in others. What is the condition of your heart in these areas and where are you in the progression of warnings?

Social: Son   1—2—3—4—5—6—7—8—9—10—11—12
Orphan

Financial: Son   1—2—3—4—5—6—7—8—9—10—11—12
Orphan

Spiritual: Son   1—2—3—4—5—6—7—8—9—10—11—12
Orphan

Physical: Son   1—2—3—4—5—6—7—8—9—10—11—12
Orphan

Mental: Son   1—2—3—4—5—6—7—8—9—10—11—12
Orphan

CHAPTER FOUR

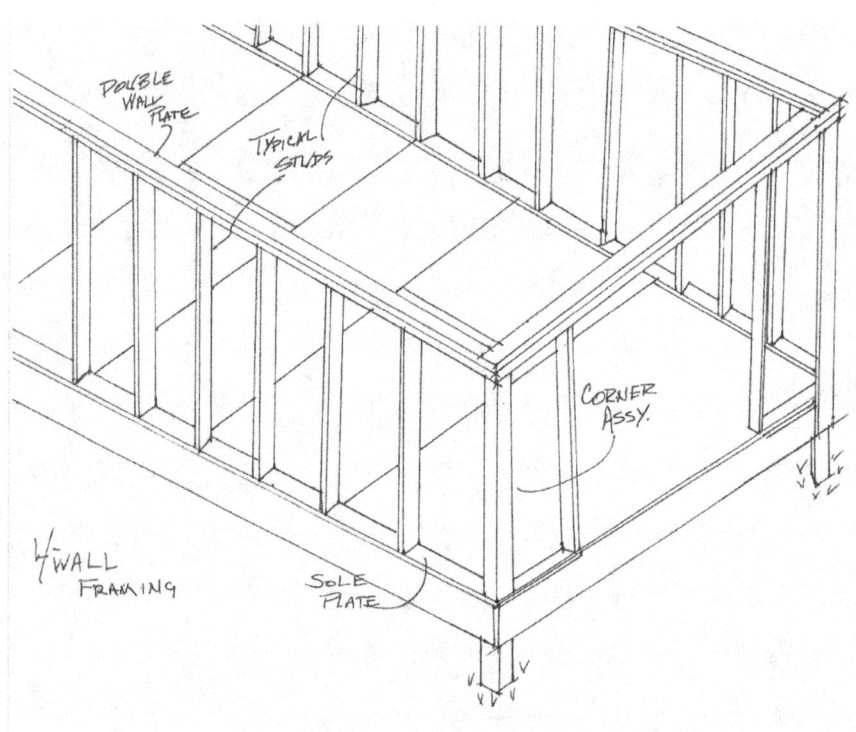

Psalm 91
The Prayer of a Warrior

> "He comforts us in all our troubles so that we can comfort others. When they are troubled, we will be able to give them the same comfort God has given us." *(2 Corinthians 1:4 NLT).*

Framing the Walls

Today, we will frame the walls and a door. We will be using the same tools we have been using. As the plans show, we will be setting studs on 16" centers. First, mark the top and bottom plates together, then measure and cut the support studs to the right length. Then we'll nail it all together. We will be making our shed walls 6' tall at the eve so we will be subtracting the width of the 3 plates (4 ½") from 72", which equals 67 ½". There will be one plate on the bottom— usually treated pine to protect from moisture and termites— and two plates on the top for strength.

There are several methods used for framing for many different reasons. For this shed, we will be assembling the walls, laying them flat on the floor, and then standing them up, leveling them, and securing the corners together. We will lay out the studs to accommodate interior sheeting. This means that in every corner, there needs to be a stud to nail/screw Sheetrock or some other sheeting to. Also, for strength, the walls overlap each other with the top plate. All of this will be explained in person when we build the walls together.

Being a Dad

When Sophia was accepted at Yale University, I was asked by several dads, "How did you do it?" My response was, "Love your kids!" I could've said that I really didn't do anything, attempting to act like I was being humble. That would lead you to believe that Sophia did it all on her own. So, you might conclude that you **can't** create an environment—at home and outside the home—which would encourage your kids to be more than you, or they, ever dreamed.

I could tell you that "God did it all!" Leading you to believe that I was again not responsible in any way. Or I could brag on what a great dad I was and that if it wasn't for me, she never would have made it to Yale. (Which is partially true. Ha ha ha!) All of these answers would lead you to draw back and neglect the absolute masterpiece of a child that **you** have living in **your** home.

You are a **DAD**! You are the most influential person in your household. You hold the positive and negative destiny of your children in your hands and in your heart! So it's how we handle the struggles at home that will etch an eternal memory and build a permanent character in your kids. Daddy, you are the key to your child's future, success, and happiness! We are told that we can make a difference in the world. I am telling you that you can make a difference at home. Your legacy is the number one God-given calling of your life.

D-A-D acronyms
Drinking and Driving
Dial A Dietician
Death And Destruction
Dark Armed Dragon

Dollar A Day
Die Another Day
Diabetic Alert Dog
Delayed After Depolarization
Days After Draining
Dogs Against Drugs

Digital Art Design
Dedicated and Devoted
Disciplined Agile Delivery
Director of Admissions
Downtown Arts District
Database Application Developer
Defense Accounts Department
Divide and Delegate
Deputy Assistant Director
Direct Access Democracy
Dispense As Directed
Disaster Assistance Director
Decide Announce Defend

Pick out your favorite description! You are a **DAD**! If you don't have kids, you are still a **DAD** to someone!

So, love the good in your kids. Love the bad in your kids. What if Father has a plan to turn that "bad" character into a world-shaking, awesome character?

Support them.

Redeem them

Protect them.

Patiently fight for them.

Comfort them.

Encourage the hell out of them–Empower them to choose well.

Love your kids like this, and they will love you. Appreciate every characteristic of their personality. Help them develop their personality into the final product God intended. Prayerfully encourage them to make the decisions they can make on their own. Praise them when they choose right and instruct and comfort them when they choose wrong.

Are you qualified for this mammoth of a responsibility? No! You don't need to be! Just say "Yes to the Call! Pray like this, "With Your help, Father, I am going to be the best Dad I can be, today! And if I mess up, I'll start all over! But I promise that I will not stop trying! Ever! Amen!"

How's it going at home?
Last time we talked about our option to choose the path of an orphan or the path of a son. We talked about how the experiences and choices we have faced define what Love is and how Love works in our lives. We know who our Father is—The Loving Creator of All Things. We know God sees us as His very own Son, made in His image, a masterpiece in His hands, being formed and perfected every day. We are learning the depth, width, and height of God's love for us. So how has that been going? Has it been kind of Rough? Tedious? Have you had lots of failures? Are you thinking that it's going to take forever and you'll never get it? It's ok! Welcome to the process of building relationships.

Like driving from the plains to the mountains, the closer you get, the bigger this gets. Our Heavenly Father is infinite! The more you learn, the more there is to learn. So be patient with yourself. Don't judge others or try to correct anyone's faulty beliefs just yet. Everything is new and very fragile. The heart of a Son, like a new plant sprouting, needs water, food, and protection until its roots grow so deep into Father's love that it cannot be moved.

For the moment, focus on your relationship with your Heavenly Father and **BEING** a really good Son! Focus on realigning and improving all your beliefs about Father and Yourself. Remind yourself daily of all the things we have talked about. Work on loving others, not because it's a requirement, but because your Heavenly Father loves you and gives you plenty of Love to give.

"Don't let your hearts be troubled. Trust in God, and trust also in me. There is more than enough room in my Father's home. If this were not so, would I have told you that I am going to prepare a place for you? When everything is ready, I will come and get you, so that you will always be with me where I am." (John 14:1-3 NLT).

Today, we are going to learn how Our Loving Father defends and protects us because we are His very own! This is what will make us **"DAD"** to our kids, and the King riding a white horse to rescue our wives. This revelation of how Father protects us will empower us to protect ourselves and our family.

The Secret Place

When I was in college, I studied under a master of prayer, Dr Larry Lea. One summer, I regularly attended his church, and I would go to his early morning prayer meetings. Here is where I learned how to pray the Lord's Prayer, the way Jesus prayed. I began to get up and pray every morning with the spiritual maturity and discipline I had at the time. After years of walking out that revelation, I began to feel a hunger for a deeper knowledge of God. That's when I got a first-level revelation of Psalm 91 and the Secret Place. Today I'm going to share that foundational revelation with you.

Moses was the Author

This Psalm was written by Moses. An adopted son of Pharaoh, trained by his father and raised to be a great leader, a prince, and a mighty warrior. But he was also an orphan. Abandoned by his mother to save his life. At the time of Moses' birth, Pharaoh was having all the Hebrew babies killed. He commanded them to be thrown into the Nile River to be eaten by the alligators. But he was rescued by the daughter of Pharaoh and raised in the palace as a prince. Later, he would escape Egypt only to be confronted by God in the desert.

Moses was the only person to talk with God face-to-face. Moses spent some 40 days alone with God up on a mountain. Moses understood what the Secret Place was and what happened when He spent time there. Out of that experience, he wrote Psalm 91. In this psalm, four people are speaking. First is the Holy Spirit, second is the Man of Faith, third is Jesus, and fourth is God, our Father. It's important to know who is speaking so we can better understand what is being said.

Psalm 91

Whoever dwells in the shelter of the Most High will rest in the shadow of the Almighty.

I will say of the Lord, "He is my refuge and my fortress, my God, in whom I trust."

Surely he will save you from the fowler's snare and from the deadly pestilence.

He will cover you with his feathers, and under his wings you will find refuge; his truth will be your shield and buckler.

You will not fear the terror of night, nor the arrow that flies by day, nor the pestilence that stalks in the darkness, nor the plague that destroys at midday.

A thousand may fall at your side, ten thousand at your right hand, but it will not come near you.

You will only observe with your eyes and see the punishment of the wicked.

If you say, "The Lord is my refuge," and you make the Most High your dwelling, no harm will overtake you, no disaster will come near your tent. For he will command his angels concerning you to guard you in all your ways; they will lift you in their hands, so that you will not strike your foot against a stone. You will tread on the lion and the cobra; you will trample the great lion and the serpent.

"Because he loves me," says the Lord, "I will rescue him; I will protect him, for he acknowledges my name. He will call on me, and I will answer him; I will be with him in trouble, I will deliver him and honor him. With long life I will satisfy him and show him my salvation." (Psalms 91:1-16 NIV).

Let's go deeper
Verse 1

He that dwells in the Secret Place of the Most High God, shall abide under the shadow of the Almighty.

This is the voice of the Holy Spirit announcing to mankind the existence of The Secret Place and the choice we have to enter into it. He says that we can live here, at home, protected and safe with our Heavenly Father. He is speaking to the Sons of God. Of course, Father is always with us. Remember, in the Garden of Eden, Father leaving His kids was not the problem. Kids leaving Father was the problem! So we need to learn how to live aware of His presence every minute of every day. Although, like you have special times just talking with your wife or your kids, this time in the Secret Place is a special time with God.

In The Secret Place, you can expose the most wounded parts of your heart without being criticized or judged. In The Secret Place you will be given Wisdom and Healing. This needs to become a vital part of our everyday life.

Moses was taught by God how to enter this place physically but also (and most importantly), spiritually. In this place, your enemy cannot find you. This is a place where we LIVE! Not just a closet where we spend 5 minutes or even 6 hours. It's where we live! It's a state of mind. It's the place where your heart rests. It's Home for your spirit. It's being aware of your Heavenly Father being with you all the time. This requires discipline. Where are you living now?

Our flesh fights to live in imaginations of pleasure without discipline.

Our enemy gives us false comfort and false security, which is designed to drag us into fear that attempts to control our every thought. Our hearts long for the safe home of The Secret Place. Moses knew how to dwell here. He spent many days there with God. What an amazing experience.

In The Secret Place, there are 2 places to live. One is The Secret Place where we dwell or live. This is our home. Home is where you eat, play, rest, and recover from the day. Home is warm, inviting, and open to encouraging conversation, instruction, education, and laughter. Home is also not perfect. That's ok. This void of perfection opens space for creativity and adventure. Now, you might be thinking, "That this is not how my home is right now." I have good news and better news! The atmosphere in your home is a reflection of the condition of your heart. That was the good news. Now you know the condition of your heart. The better news is that it can always be fixed and changed! It always starts with us, **DADS**!

The second place is Under the Shadow of the Almighty. Now really, God—being Light—cannot cast a shadow. He is talking about His position, which is looking over you. He is your protector and your comforter. He is watching over you all the time, not allowing issues to arise higher than you can handle.

"No temptation has overtaken you except what is common to mankind. And God is faithful; he will not let you be tempted beyond what you can bear. But when you are tempted, he will also provide a way out so that you can endure it." (1 Corinthians 10:13 NIV).

The Amplified Bible reads this way:

…Will remain secure and rest in the shadow of the Almighty [whose power no enemy can withstand].

Your Heavenly Father is the Most Mighty, and no enemy can get to you here in the Secret Place. You are safe and secure here. When you feel overwhelmed, it is here that fear has to go! (Love conquers all fear. 1 John 4:18) It's here that we can hear Father talk with us softly (1 Kings 19:12) in the middle of disaster, terror, and even certain death. Here is where our faith is built, our mouth confesses, and salvation comes swooping down to save us (Romans 10:9). This is where we win our battles before they begin (Exodus 17:10-16)! This is The Secret Place, the Home of Almighty God and His Favorite Son, YOU! Be determined to live there and see what happens.

The next person we hear is the voice of the Believer—The Son—who chooses to trust in his Father and makes his statement of faith.

Verse 2
I will say of the Lord, "He is my refuge and my fortress; My God, in Him I will trust."

Today, as I write this section of the curriculum, I can tell you that yesterday I was faced with a very disappointing situation. I was offended, personally hurt, disappointed, and felt that it was all my fault. I lost, I failed, and there was nothing that could be done about it. Then I remembered the declaration that I make almost daily. It's not exactly Psalm 91:2, but the same idea. Because of that practice, it was what came up out of my spirit instinctively. And I said out loud, "You are My Heavenly Father and You are my Provider! Your perfect will is being done in my life, and I don't care what it looks like. You take care of me and I depend on You and not on anything else!" And guess what happened? Nothing yet! Except inside, I was free! I was back in the Secret Place with My Father and under His care again. Now I can continue with my day with a clear head and a strong heart instead of a confused head and a defeated heart. A few hours later, the whole thing got fixed.

Was it luck or a coincidence? I don't think so! Was I overreacting? Maybe. Probably. Maybe it was all going to turn out that way anyway. All I know is that time after time, things work out in my favor and they don't work out for others. I would rather take the Faith path and see more favorable results than unfavorable results. How about you?

This statement is a declaration of Faith made by the Man who has chosen the Creator to be His Heavenly Father, just like I did yesterday. We declare, by faith, that Father is "our place" to go for shelter and help and that we will not turn to anywhere else for shelter, comfort, or help. We will be trusting in Father and nothing else. We choose the Father of all Creation to be our place of refuge and protection. A safe place where we can run when we are afraid, angry, confused, or tired. This is where we turn and run to! Not the desires of our flesh and the carnal comforts of pleasure without discipline.

I will say of the Lord, "He is my refuge and my fortress; My God, in Him I will trust."

The next few verses are the voice of Jesus! **He** has trusted in **His** Father, and from **His** experience, **He** declares what **has** happened when **He** trusted in **His** Father and what **will** happen if **we** trust in **His** Father. As we go through every verse, let this truth sink in and renew your mind and grow your faith.

Verse 3
Surely He shall deliver you from the snare of the fowler and from the perilous pestilence.

A snare is a wire or rope made into a slip loop. It's designed to be hidden or disguised so the bird doesn't see it. Then, when he steps into the snare, it catches his leg by the foot, and he cannot escape. I have seen this so many times. When I spend time with my Father in the Secret Place, He warns me of hidden, coming troubles, the traps set by my enemy. Many times, I have spent some time with Father talking about a certain job or adventure I want to go on. I try to wait for the "go" or "no go". This has helped me avoid numerous unforeseeable attacks. Of course, things have happened, and I have gotten caught, but He always shows me the way out when others are freaking out and don't know what to do. Honestly, it results in a somewhat boring, testimonial life. But! Would you rather have that or a life filled with chaos and troubles, which Father is constantly delivering you from? I choose boring.

Pestilence refers to all kinds of spiritual and natural bugs. Things that won't quit harassing you all day long. Declaring your trust in Him and remaining in or returning to the Secret Place neutralizes and protects us from pestilence! I use this verse on bacteria, viruses, mosquitoes, and lately, wasps. It really does work.

Verse 4
He shall cover you with His feathers, and under His wings you shall take refuge.

Referring to the hen covering her very vulnerable chicks with her wings, The Secret Place is where we run when danger lurks. Like the hen, when we(as the chicks)are oblivious to imminent dangers, Father knows when to call us to Himself so He can cover us and protect us. Where do we run when we are afraid or discouraged? Run to the Father! He is our Refuge!

Verse 4

His truth shall be your shield and buckler.

He is the Truth, the Way, and the Life! No one comes to the Father except through the Son, Jesus! (John 14:6) Truth is like a shield. When we know what is true, we will know a lie or a counterfeit when we see it. The Truth protects us from lies, which only harm us.

Truth is also like a belt. Soldiers wear a belt which holds their tools and their weapons. All of your weapons of faith, which you can use on your enemy, the devil, will hang (or depend upon or be derived from) the Truth! Remember, even Pilate asked Jesus about the Truth.

"Pilate therefore said to Him, 'Are You a king then?' Jesus answered, 'You say rightly that I am a king. For this cause I was born, and for this cause I have come into the world, that I should bear witness to the truth. Everyone who is of the truth hears My voice.' Pilate said to Him, 'What is truth?' And when he had said this, he went out again to the Jews, and said to them, 'I find no fault in Him at all.'" (John 18:37-38 NKJV).

What is the truth? Jesus is the Truth. There is only one who knows what is real and what is fake, what is all true and what is truth that is twisted. Your Heavenly Father is the only one who knows the truth about anything and everything. So when we turn to Him in The Secret Place, we will find the truth! When we know the Truth about something, the Truth we know will protect us from lies and set us free.

Verse 5-6
You shall not be afraid of the terror by night,
Nor of the arrow that flies by day,
Nor of the pestilence that walks in darkness,
Nor of the destruction that lays waste at noonday.

There is no fear in the Secret Place. I hear all the time about people who cannot sleep. And there are many reasons for this. My baby granddaughter woke up every few hours at night, waking my daughter. That's normal. When we are about to go on vacation, my wife, Claudia, many times can't sleep because she is so excited. That's ok. When I was in college, I would come home from work at 1 am and couldn't sleep because I was so pumped up from work. That's normal. I would eat a big candy bar and pass out. But Worry and fear—the terror of the night—is different.

I used to be rigidly afraid of the dark. As a teenager, I would pee in my bed because I was so afraid to get up in the dark, by myself, and go to the bathroom. But when I got saved and asked Jesus into my heart at 15 years old, He obliterated my fear of the dark. If the night tortures you, go spend some time in The Secret Place and watch the fear leave.

Some things—in the cover of darkness—attack us when we can't see them. It's a great warfare tactic to attack at night. But also, things come at us during the day like arrows. All we hear is the swish of the air immediately before feeling the pierce of the arrow. Not even animals can react quickly enough to dodge an arrow. But in The Secret Place, we have peace because we have protection—The One watching over us all the time?

It is interesting that, again, Moses speaks of bugs and dangers in the dark cover of night and in the clear sight of daylight. Dangers worthy of fear from every direction. Only in the Secret Place can we find protection, comfort, and peace.

Verse 7
A thousand may fall at your side,
And ten thousand at your right hand;

This is common with experienced soldiers. When we are in a battle, we will see our own friends—hundreds of brothers, sisters, fathers, and mothers—falling right beside us. They may be more talented, intelligent, trained, experienced, or wise than us, but they get hit. We don't know why. It is difficult to endure death; we were not designed for it. We were designed for Life. It is especially difficult to endure the death of someone we love and respect.

Then, to add injury to insult, there are the tens of thousands of enemies that we must kill with our own hands! Maybe you had to end a marriage because of abuse that would not end any other way. Maybe you had to end a friendship that was poisonous to your life of faith. Maybe you are or were a soldier in the military and had to physically kill someone. Either way, the death of even our enemies at our hands is a horrible thing to endure.

As for all those who have died, I refuse to judge them and say it was because they were not in their Secret Place. But I will say, "IT WILL NOT COME NEAR ME!"

Verse 7
But it shall not come near you.

There are those enemies that I can put a stop to, and there are those who are fighting beside me—all falling in the battle. I don't know about everyone else, but I know that when I put my trust in My Father, in The Secret Place, death will not come near me. This is my confidence when I am afraid. Others give us the statistics, averages, and probabilities of an outcome, but my Heavenly Father does not operate in the realm of averages and probabilities. He sees the end from the beginning (Isaiah 46:10). He knows where He wants me and when He wants me to be there. So I don't live under the confidence of success or the fear of the disaster of those around me. I live by the instructions and directions of My Father, which I received in the Peaceful Home of The Secret Place.

Verse 8
Only with your eyes shall you look,
And see the reward of the wicked.

I've heard many people say that only by experiencing someone's pain can we understand what they are going through, and so be able to help them. That may be somewhat true, but I don't need to become an alcoholic to know that it's a bad life to live! I can see with my eyes the destruction that person is causing in his life and everyone around him. In The Secret Place, I can see the result of others' decisions and decide which way to go without having to suffer the painful consequences. Why do I only see the disaster others are causing by their decisions? Because I am protected by My Father in The Secret Place.

Verse 9-13
Because you have made the Lord, who is My refuge,
Even the Most High, your dwelling place,
No evil shall befall you,
Nor shall any plague come near your dwelling;
For He shall give His angels charge over you,
To keep you in all your ways.
In their hands they shall bear you up,
Lest you dash your foot against a stone.
You shall tread upon the lion and the cobra,
The young lion and the serpent you shall trample underfoot.

In verse 9, you can see that it is Jesus who is talking. He is stating that He conquered sin and death by remaining in The Secret Place! He is telling us that if He did it this way, we can too. What an awesome God we serve, that He would prove out His way of doing things to show us that we can do it too.

Again, no evil or sickness will come into our house. This is a great thing to claim over our house. When everyone seems to be getting sick, we can speak and claim by faith, over our house, that no plague can enter here.

This next verse mentions angels. Angels are real. I always believe my Father protects me, but for some reason, He gives that job to angels too. So when you feel led by the Holy Spirit, you can command the angels to watch over you, too. It's all through the Bible. Angels delivered messages, fought battles, and protected prophets. Angels will help us too if we tell them.

Then the last part talks about walking on lions and snakes. Don't go out and handle snakes and lions unless you know what you are doing. For example: YOU WORK AT THE ZOO AND THAT'S YOUR PROFESSION OR YOUR JOB! But like Paul—in Acts 28:3–was accidentally bitten by a snake and didn't die when he should've. He was probably standing on Psalm 91:13 when that happened! When we live in The Secret Place, we can do things that are usually not possible. This is the message of this verse. We do not always operate under the rules of death. We live above the grave! Jesus was given authority over heaven and earth (Matthew 28:18-19) and then told us to GO! So we GO under His authority and have the choice to live above the grave.

Live in The Secret Place! And when you think it couldn't possibly get better than this! Hold onto your chair! It gets better.

The next voice is the Father commenting on how He sees our move of faith.

Verse 14-16
Because he has set his love upon Me,
therefore I will deliver him;
I will set him on high,
because he has known My name.
He shall call upon Me, and I will answer him;
I will be with him in trouble;
I will deliver him and honor him.
With long life I will satisfy him,
And show him My salvation.

Now we can see how important Love and Trust are to God! When we set our Love on Him and trust in Him, resting in The Secret Place, He will rescue us and put us in a safe place out of harm's way because we believed in His Love for us as His very own Kids! Notice Father is very clear to say that we have a part and He has a part. He is resolute and excited to do His part, so He is very clear about what we need to do.

First, set your Love on Him. Decide to trust in Him and be dependent on Him and nothing else. Just like when your kids turn away from what they are doing and run to you. Think about it, if one of your kids gets hurt and instead of turning to you for help, they just hide and act like nothing happened, how will they ever heal? Just as our little ones don't know how to take care of themselves properly, we don't know how to take care of ourselves properly. Our first priority is to turn to Him and recognize His Name or His Character and choose to love Him because He loved us first.

The second priority is to **call on Him** or ask Him for help. Romans 10:10 says that we first believe in our heart, then we ask, and then we will be saved. If we ask but we don't really believe He loves us, only because of His great mercy, might we get something. But if we set our Love on Him and ask, He will answer us, manifest Himself, deliver us, and satisfy us during our long life. If you read through the Old Testament, you will see this time after time! When people turned to Father instead of themselves for comfort and answers, He rescued them every time. He will do the same for us!

Notice that Father keeps stating that when we are in trouble, He will rescue us. Why are we in trouble when Jesus said that living in the Secret Place would keep us out of trouble? Because we live in a dark world full of trouble, and our job is to be an example of Christ in the midst of the troubles. Even Jesus had troubles for this same reason! He had troubles with his family, troubles with the religious church people, troubles with His own disciples, and troubles with the weather. He told us that we will have troubles and persecutions too. But Jesus knew how to handle it all—from within The Secret Place. And He is telling us how to do exactly what He did!

Father says that He will be with us when we are in trouble. Our Heavenly Father NEVER leaves us. Even when we are going through a difficult and painful time, He will be there, feeling all that pain with us, giving us wisdom, giving us strength, and protecting us along the way.

Remember the story of Shadrach, Meshach, and Abednego? Daniel 3 tells the story of how three Jewish boys refused to bow down and worship the golden idol. Father didn't prevent them from going into the fire. He had a plan to do more than rescue those boys. Father wanted to impact King Nebuchadnezzar so greatly that he would have a change of heart and actually care for all the people of Israel. And what did the king see in the fire?

"Look!" he answered, "I see four men loose, walking in the midst of the fire; and they are not hurt, and the form of the fourth is like the Son of God." (Daniel 3:25 NKJV).

He saw someone amazing! Maybe Jesus, walking around in the fire with those boys! Father saved those boys and made a huge statement before the king! That's why we go through troubles. To be a huge witness to believers and unbelievers around us. So when we are going through something horrible, Father is right there and He has a plan! We don't give up on Him and start crying and asking, "Why am I going through this?" We trust in Him, we make Him our refuge, we stay in The Secret Place with Him, and we will see Him work!

Our Heavenly Father honors our trust in Him, which comes from our Love for Him. He desires to satisfy us with a long, happy life, full of joy and peace and Blessing! But the best part is that He will reveal His Son, Jesus, our Savior, to us.

What a life we have! The opportunity to live under the shadow of His wings, The Secret Place, the Home of the Creator of All Things and His Sons.

The Secret Place can also be compared to an umbrella. As long as we stay under the umbrella, we won't get wet. But if we get out from under the umbrella, wet we will get! Enter into the Secret Place where only You and Father can occupy! It's a sacred place for a Father and His son.

Questions:

What was the coolest thing you learned today, building the walls?
_____
_____

What verse in Psalm 91 helps you the most today?
_____
_____

What verse in Psalm 91 do you want to work on the most?
_____
_____

Where, specifically, will you use what you learned today from Psalm 91 this week?
_____
_____

CHAPTER FIVE

5 - ROOF FRAMING

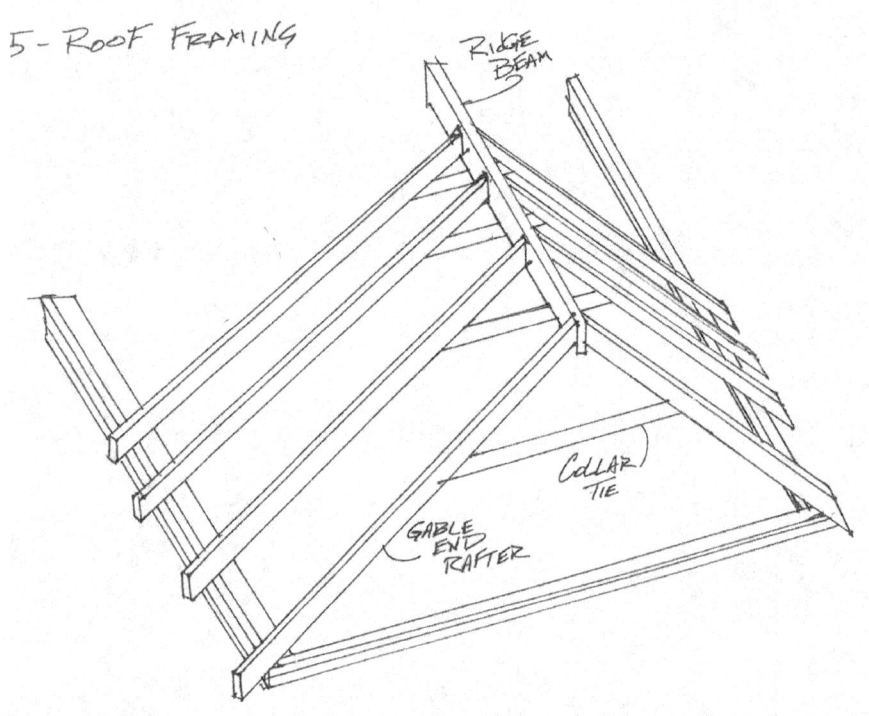

The Armor of God!
The Shelter of the Most High God

"Put on all of God's armor so that you will be able to stand firm against all strategies of the devil."
(Ephesians 6:10 NLT)

Build the Roof!

In this session, we will build the trusses for the roof and set them on top of the walls. Trusses take a little different kind of planning. We will have to use some forethought, common sense, and some fancy math. Also, we'll learn how to make a jig for the design of the trusses. To assemble and install the trusses on the walls of the shed, it will require several men, so we will have to work as a team.

We will be building a 3/12 pitch, gabled roof. This means that there will be a peak in the middle, sloping straight to the walls on either side. 4/12 pitch means that for every 12" the rafter travels horizontally, the roofline will rise 4". Since our shed is 8' wide, the peak of the roof is 4' from the outside wall. So in the center we will have a rise of 16". Using our speed square, we will determine, mark, and cut the top angle of the rafters on the 4/12 pitch mark. We will calculate the length of the rafter by finding the hypotenuse of this right triangle and adding 6" for overhang.

$A^2+B^2=C^2$. $56^2+16^2=72"$

C is the roof line or the longest side of the triangle, which will be 72"

Under the peak, there will be a collar tie (see the picture above), which helps distribute the weight so the roof doesn't push the walls out. We will build the collar ties from siding scraps, which we will cut to size and shape, glue, and then staple in place. This will create a nice, strong roof, able to hold up under a good snow load for the Oklahoma climate.

We will be setting each rafter over the corresponding wall stud, 16" on center. We will overhang 6" on the side walls. We will build the trusses on the ground and then lift them into place and nail them to the walls. Then we will build the end walls up to the roof line.

We will also build the rafters to accommodate a ridge beam. A ridge beam is a 2x4 that spans from front to back at the peak of the rafters. This holds the rafters in place and creates a nice, strong ridge across the top.

Like a roof, the Armor of God is a covering. It also requires structure, design, and repetition, resulting in a strong covering and shelter from the elements.

Hearts Under Construction

Imagine your enemy coming at you with all his fury, sneaking up from behind with a plan to absolutely destroy you. But when you turn around, he sees God! What would you do if you were that enemy? I'd run! Your enemy will not act scared, but he is! He knows exactly what will happen to him when a Son of God wears (and knows how to use) the clothes of The Son of God.

Our Current Condition

"In that day seven women will take hold of one man and say, 'We will eat our own food and provide our own clothes; only let us be called by your name. Take away our disgrace!'" (Isaiah 4:1 NIV).

Ordinarily, in marriage, a man would provide his wife with food and clothes, and she would take his name, forsaking hers. They would enjoy a new life together, benefiting each other. But in this situation, the women are only asking to be rescued from disgrace. They want to be rescued from their troubles—as a good husband would—but without the relationship with him. They don't want the clothes he would normally give to her to wear. He would also give her food, but they are saying that they will find their own food too. This is a very one-sided relationship reflecting, prophetically, the mentality of the modern-day Church.

According to prophecy, seven is the number of completion or referring to something whole. The "women" who want to marry one man refers to the Bride of Christ—which is the Church— and Jesus would be the man they wish to marry. The food they should be receiving from Him is the Word of God or Jesus, who is the Bread of Life. The clothes they refused to wear are His clothes, which represent Him. They do want to take His Name, but only for appearance, so they are not disgraced before people. They only want to do what is required so they may escape death, but they want to create their own appearance and feed from their own knowledge. So when we look at this prophetically, we can see a very one-sided relationship we are tempted to desire. Another perfect description of the Orphan Heart.

As Sons of God, our food is Jesus, the Word of God, the Bread of Life, which He is. The clothes that we should be wearing are the Armor of God outlined in Ephesians 6. We need His food, but we also need His clothing! Our enemy knows what he can do when we are spiritually naked. He can deceive us, manipulate us, damage our hearts, and destroy us. He is the god of this world, but he is NOT our Father unless we choose him.

Jesus paid the price and took the keys of hell and the grave and gave us His authority over spiritual bullies trying to take us by surprise. When we read the letter written to the Ephesians, especially chapter six, we can see clearly that our daily issues are with people, and our battle is **not** with people! Our battle is also not with things on the earth like earthquakes, wind, the sun, or rain. Those things are not really out to hurt us. We don't even fight animals. They're not really trying to hurt us. We don't need to always fight people. Sometimes we must, but first we should defend ourselves and attack spiritually. We cannot change people, and we don't need to be manipulating people. So who are we fighting?

"Put on all of God's armor so that you will be able to stand firm against all strategies of the devil. For we are not fighting against flesh-and-blood enemies, but against evil rulers and authorities of the unseen world, against mighty powers in this dark world, and against evil spirits in the heavenly places." (Ephesians 6:11-12 NLT).

It's not people and things we fight, but what is influencing many and controlling some.

The Armor of God—Jesus' clothes—protects us from spiritual attacks and empowers us to fight the source of the problem—unseen, dark, spiritual forces. The Armor of God empowers us to deal with those forces that are acting through people to steal, kill, and destroy us. They attempt to deceive us into believing lies and acting on things that are not true, causing our own destruction. It is not people we fight, but the forces that work through people. With the Armor of God, we can know the truth so we can effectively do the right things, defend our hearts, vet our thoughts, guard against temptations, and fight back with Father's promises to us.

That's what we are going to learn about today. Paul, under the influence of the Holy Spirit, did an excellent job of giving us a list of weapons that we need to use. Each part of a soldier's armor is a great example of our spiritual clothing. We just need to know how to use it, and when the time comes, remember to use it. So here we go.

"Finally, be strong in the Lord and in his mighty power. Put on the full armor of God, so that you can take your stand against the devil's schemes. For our struggle is not against flesh and blood, but against the rulers, against the authorities, against the powers of this dark world and against the spiritual forces of evil in the heavenly realms. Therefore, put on the full armor of God, so that when the day of evil comes, you may be able to stand your ground, and after you have done everything, to stand. Stand firm then, with the belt of truth buckled around your waist, with the breastplate of righteousness in place, and with your feet fitted with the readiness that comes from the gospel of peace. In addition to all this, take up the shield of faith, with which you can extinguish all the flaming arrows of the evil one. Take the helmet of salvation and the sword of the Spirit, which is the word of God." (Ephesians 6:10-17).

Purpose for the armor.

If you read all of chapter 6, you will see Paul's reason for establishing this truth about the Armor of God. Its main function is to empower us to deal with people and act like Jesus would! Father's armor is spiritual and designed for a spiritual battle. Our goal is to overcome spiritual resistance first, before anything physical comes to pass. Adam was given the chance to fight his spiritual battle when Father asked him what had happened. If Adam fought his battle spiritually first, I believe he would have asked for forgiveness, Father would have forgiven him (because that is what love does), and the story in the Bible would be very different. Adam may have been recorded as the Father of Faith, like Abraham was labeled later. Forever we would be recalling that we have great faith because Adam believed in Father's love and Father forgave him! Wow! What a foundational belief to stand on.

We are not so familiar with armor, but in the days of Paul, when this was written, they were very familiar with this sort of thing. This was the way the Romans wore their armor.

The Belt of Truth

"Jesus answered, 'I am the way and the truth and the life. No one comes to the Father except through me.'" (John 14:6 NIV).

"Do your best to present yourself to God as one approved, a worker who does not need to be ashamed and who correctly handles the word of truth." (2 Timothy 2:15 NIV).

"For the law was given through Moses; grace and truth came through Jesus Christ."
(John 1:17 NIV).

A Roman soldier's belt would hold everything together. It held the sheath for their sword, maybe a knife, and any other weapons they might have. Everything hung on that belt. A belt is also a tool that holds your muscles together in your abdomen. Weightlifters wear a belt to keep from blowing out stomach muscles.

Since the Word of God is the Truth, it is the standard for what we should believe. I believe it is vitally important to often reconsider what we believe. That is why we spent a week asking Father to reveal to us something we thought was true, and it wasn't. It just works out all the lies we have been taught over the years. That's one thing I really despise. Believing something is true and finding out it wasn't! It makes me feel so vulnerable to deception and so very free at the same time.

Truth is the foundation for everything we do. Our life can be a twisted-up mess only because our beliefs are twisted and weak. True Faith—which comes from God—can only attach itself to something that is True. If someone tells you that they deposited a million dollars in your bank account, but they didn't(this is the lie), it won't matter how much you believe it and try to withdraw it; you won't get any out. This may cause you to get all stressed out, especially if you make decisions based on the lie that you had enough money in your account. This is actually fear at work. Fear is faith linked to a lie. Or believing in a lie.

Faith in God is believing in something true about God. When we settle and establish our faith in a Truth about God, that Truth we know will set us free when we are face to face with our enemy. All of us (and the worst of us) got Born Again when we believed one Truth about our Heavenly Father. That Truth came in the form of a scripture.

What was the Truth, or the scripture, that you heard which led you to faith in Jesus when you got Born Again?

_____

_____

If we get into a real big battle with the enemy and our faith is rattled, we can sit down and remind ourselves of that scripture and what happened. This is the foundation of our faith, and the Truth of that scripture will revive and empower us to overcome.

As we grow in Christ, there are other scriptures that will become foundational Truths which we can lean on or trust in when we are in trouble. These revelations of Truth, which we know, we tightly buckle around everything we believe. We make all our decisions from these Truths. So it's the Truth that makes us strong. Jesus is the Truth, and we choose every day to receive Him as the Truth in our lives. We clothe ourselves in Him—our Truth.

Then we determine to deny all lies. Lies come all the time, so when we acknowledge Him as The Truth, we can see a lie when it comes.

Imagine girding The Truth around yourself like a big weight-lifting belt. Say, " I declare today: I know the truth and the truth that I know will set me free. I resist and deny all lies. And I can see a lie a mile away! My enemy is the father of all lies, and I am not his son! I am a Child of The Truth!"

The Breastplate of Righteousness

Therefore, if any man be in Christ, he is a new creature: old things are passed away; behold, all things are become new (v.17). For he hath made him to be sin for us, who knew no sin; that we might be made the righteousness of God in him (v.21). (2 Corinthians 5:17-21).

"Therefore, since we have been made right in God's sight by faith, we have peace with God because of what Jesus Christ our Lord has done for us. Because of our faith, Christ has brought us into this place of undeserved privilege where we now stand, and we confidently and joyfully look forward to sharing God's glory." (Romans 5:1-2 NLT).

"For if by one man's offence death reigned by one…even so by the righteousness of one the free gift came upon all men unto justification of life. For as by one man's disobedience many were made sinners, so by the obedience of one shall many be made righteous." (Romans 5:17-19).

Do you want to perfect your relationship with God? Develop your faith in righteousness—your "right" standing with Him. Our right standing with God is vital to our successful existence. Because it is so important, it is also an area that our enemy ruthlessly attacks! He attacks our right standing with God so much because when we know where we stand with God, the enemy is powerless to weaken our resolve.

The breastplate of a Roman soldier's armor covered his front. It protected all of his vital organs. Right Standing with Father protects all the vital functions of our spirit, and it only comes by faith. Our belief in the Righteousness given to us by Jesus' dying on the cross is the strength of our foundational beliefs. He paid the price for us to have a Place Beside our Heavenly Father! Standing Right Beside Him!

Think about that for a minute. If we face an enemy more powerful than we are, by ourselves, he might feel very confident that he can take us out. But if someone —much greater than he—is standing right beside us, he knows he is about to get pounded if he attacks! And you know that even if he does attack, Father, standing right beside you, will defend you.

We need to establish our faith in the Blood of Jesus and our right standing with God. This is a great example: We can **believe** that we have a million dollars in the bank, because we do. But if we don't **believe** that we have the **right** to withdraw some of it when we want, it won't do us any good.

If we don't believe we can use what we have, we are defeated already.

The enemy will attack us with a goal to convince us that we don't have the right standing with our Father and that we don't deserve it. The Truth is that we do have righteousness only by faith in the completed work of redemption performed by Jesus. And the other Truth is that WE DON'T deserve it!

That "I need to deserve it" thinking comes from the orphan heart. An orphan has to earn his own righteousness by doing good things, completing his checklist, and obeying all the rules. It's impossible to earn right standing with God! So the orphan thinks, "I can't stand with God!" And Jesus' response is, "Adam did! And that's how we were created! To stand beside our Creator—Our Heavenly Father—with confidence and authority!" The armor makes us look like God! And reminds us and our enemy that we have been made like God through the blood of Jesus.

"For He (Father) has made Him (Jesus) to be sin for us, who knew no sin; that we might be made the righteousness of God in Him." (2 Corinthians 5:21).

Say this: "I have been made the Righteousness of God in Christ. By faith, I have full rights and authority to stand beside my Heavenly Father with confidence! Today I say "YES" to His perfect will for my life and will do only what my Father leads me to do.

Thank You, Father, for always standing by me and by my faith. You grant me Right Standing through the death and resurrection of Jesus.

My feet fit with the readiness which comes from the Gospel of Peace.

"Preach the word; be prepared in season and out of season; correct, rebuke and encourage—with great patience and careful instruction." (2 Timothy 4:2 NIV).

"But in your hearts revere Christ as Lord. Always be prepared to give an answer to everyone who asks you to give the reason for the hope that you have. But do this with gentleness and respect..." (1 Peter 3:15 NIV).

The Gospel Paul is referring to is the Good News of Jesus coming as our Messiah and our Savior, who took all our sins, sicknesses, weaknesses, and fears. He picked us up out of our bloody mess, cleaned us off, and gave us His own clothes to wear. This act of setting us free is our constant motivation for sharing what we know with whomever crosses our path.

I have the confidence to share the freedom I have with others because I remind myself that I am motivated to do what He would have me do by what He did. Like shoes on my feet, my motivations are covered, insulated, and protected by what I know Jesus has done for me and through me.

We declare: Today, I am ready in season and out of season to share the Gospel everywhere I go and as You lead me. I am motivated only by Love and compassion and not out of any selfish reasons or pride. I am ready and prepared to be a light to the world today as I was created to be. I will run this race and finish my course.

I take up the Shield of Faith and extinguish all the flaming arrows of the evil one.

When we live by Truth, powered by Righteousness, and motivated by The Gospel, we become a light to the world and a target for our enemy. So we'd better hold strong to what we **believe in**! It's the Truths that we **Believe in** that protect us from attacks from our enemy. Many of these attacks come through thoughts bombarding our minds all day. All the other attacks come from people expressing, defending, and superimposing what they believe on us and our current situation.

Truth holds everything together, Righteousness empowers our vital beliefs, and the Gospel motivates us, but our Faith defends against attacks.

Our Faith is our defense for all forward spiritual movement. Faith is the "**eye**" of our heart. What we believe is what we "**see**" with our spirit. When I was sick, I **saw** myself healthy and strong. Faith protected me from the arrows of sickness. When I didn't have enough money to pay my bills or didn't feel like I had what I needed to do what Father had put on my heart to do, by faith, I **saw** myself with enough and more than I needed. Faith in God—who He is and what He wants for me— was a shield that protected me from the arrows of not enough. Then it came.

This message has been preached for years, and the use of Faith has been taught well (and badly) and received well (and badly). It's normal for this to happen, so we need to be cautious not to blindly believe everything we hear. Go study everything for yourself. Our enemy will try to twist every good thing so we can't use our faith against him.

You may have to go down to the simplest thing you can think of to find something you really believe. We talked about this when we discussed the Belt of Truth. Start with your salvation. Do you believe you are born again? Do you believe that the Spirit of God lives in your heart? Do you believe your sins have been forgiven? Even if that's all you can deeply believe in, it's ok! It's actually a super awesome first step toward God! What you have is all you need. Jesus fed 5000 with 2 fish sandwiches. He can deliver you if you can believe in one thing that's true. That's your shield against attacks!

But these arrows come with fire! And when you have several arrows in your shield, they begin to heat things up. That's when you worship and pray in the Spirit. Exhaust your knowledge of Father, thanking

Him for everything He has done for you. Your heart will open to make more room for Him, and He will give you revelation that you didn't have before! Worshipping and praying in the Spirit is the river of life-giving water, bubbling up as a river of living water out of your soul, and it puts out the fire on your shield.

Confess this: Father! I don't care what things look like. Today I will trust in You, Your love for me, and the loving Words You have spoken over me! And when my enemy attacks me, I'll stop and praise You and remind myself of all the wonderful things You have done for me! My Faith is my Shield.

I Put on the Helmet of Salvation!

"Trust in the Lord with all your heart, And lean not on your own understanding." (Proverbs 3:5 NKJV).

"But let us who live in the light be clearheaded, protected by the armor of faith and love, and wearing as our helmet the confidence of our salvation." (1 Thessalonians 5:8 NLT).

Jesus knew how to use the Helmet of Salvation.

This is how He made it through His day. He put on His armor.

"He put on righteousness as his body armor and placed the helmet of salvation on his head." (Isaiah 59:17 NLT).

"Don't copy the behavior and customs of this world, but let God transform you into a new person by changing the way you think." (Romans 12:2 NLT).

Garbage in, Garbage out!

We are bombarded by thoughts that corrupt what is true about faith, love, Jesus, ourselves, and each other! Before you were saved and had Jesus in your heart, your sinful nature ruled your thoughts. You were held hostage by fear! When Jesus came in, He began to show you what is true and right. But these things sound different than what everyone else is saying. Why? Their thoughts are still being ruled by their sinful nature, and it's everywhere. So we're going to have to fight the lies by remembering that Jesus brought us salvation by faith.

"So letting your sinful nature control your mind leads to death. But letting the Spirit control your mind leads to life and peace." (Romans 8:5-6 NLT).

"And let the peace of God rule in your hearts." (Colossians 3:15 NKJV).

"Who can know the Lord's thoughts? Who knows enough to teach him? But we understand these things, for we have the mind of Christ." (1 Corinthians 2:16 NLT).

"Those who are dominated by the sinful nature think about sinful things, but those who are controlled by the Holy Spirit think about things that please the Spirit." (Romans 8:5 NLT).

This is the truth: we have the Holy Spirit, God, Creator of all things, in our hearts. He tells us what to kick out and what to accept! This is the protection we hav,e but the Helmet of Salvation requires some work! We have to be on guard against corrupt thoughts.

"Those who are dominated by the sinful nature think about sinful things, but those who are controlled by the Holy Spirit think about things that please the Spirit." (Romans 8:5-6).

This Helmet umpires your thoughts. We all have to deal with every kind of thought every day. Good and bad thoughts come and go. We can't do much about that, but we can choose which ones we should believe and which ones we shouldn't. This is impossible for us to do. We need the Holy Spirit who can umpire our thoughts. When we set our Trust in Him, we choose to believe that He will establish the good thoughts in our hearts and minds and dissolve the bad thoughts. Just ask. If you believe, He will do it. He will take care of your thoughts and sort them out so we can receive the good ones. (This is important!) Guess what happens to the bad ones? The Holy Spirit literally dissolves them away so they do not torment us anymore. After this, you can entertain the memory of the bad thoughts, but why? Let them dissolve into nothingness where they belong.

The Helmet of Salvation will save you from the torture of bad thoughts and leave you with right thinking— The Mind of Christ!

It's a gift from God to be able to think. To remember, imagine, and solve problems in our mind is absolutely amazing! So, since thinking is a Blessing, so is the ability to think. I've found it so much easier to appreciate our ability to think and then deal with the thoughts. They can be good or bad thoughts. Either way, when we simply commit or give those thoughts to the Holy Spirit, He sorts them out for us and makes the bad ones completely powerless. When we are bombarded by bad or negative thoughts, we need to be just as diligent to deflect them to the Holy Spirit until our enemy wears out. And he will!

Confess this: Today I put on the Helmet of Salvation. I have the mind of Christ. When thoughts come my way, I will give them to You, Holy Spirit, knowing that You will give back to me the good thoughts that came from You and dissolve the bad thoughts. Thank you for umpiring my thoughts today.

Take up the Sword of the Spirit!

"For the word of God is alive and active. Sharper than any double-edged sword, it penetrates even to dividing soul and spirit, joints and marrow; it judges the thoughts and attitudes of the heart." (Hebrews 4:12 NIV).

"As the rain and the snow come down from heaven, and do not return to it without watering the earth and making it bud and flourish, so that it yields seed for the sower and bread for the eater, so is my word that goes out from my mouth: It will not return to me empty, but will accomplish what I desire and achieve the purpose for which I sent it." (Isaiah 55:10-11 NIV).

This Sword is the spoken Word of God! Notice the spelling? S-Word? I just think that's funny in English! "S" stands for Spirit and for Spoken!

Paul wrote to Timothy saying that all scripture is useful for teaching and training. (2 Tim 3:16) The Words of God will not return void and are sharp like a double-edged sword. The Word of God is our only offensive weapon. It's the only one we need. Jesus is the Word which was spoken and manifested by the Holy Spirit! With His words, Father also spoke and created everything. So everything created falls under the authority and rule of Father's Words, which we can use as He did. All authority and power have been given to Jesus, and He gave it to us through His death and resurrection (Matthew 28:18-20).

Use your words wisely! They are not primarily used for communication. The orphaned heart believes that words are only for communication and can be used however he wishes without negative consequences. For a Child of God, words are primarily used to create and maintain order, to rule and have authority over the creation, and then for communication.

Our battle is not with people, it's for people!

Our battle is spiritual, and we fight against spiritual forces trying to rule us with lies. This is why I like to spell this piece of armor: S-Word. The Word we Speak, coming from the Spirit of God, Our Father.

We should have our S-Word ready to apply to every and any situation that arises. When I feel like I don't have enough, I will cut poverty into pieces and force it to serve me with my S-word.

"My God shall supply all my needs according to His riches in glory!" (Philippians 4:19).

"But He was wounded for my transgressions, He was bruised for my iniquities: the chastisement of my peace was upon Him; and with His stripes I am healed." (Isaiah 53:5 KJV).

"I was made the righteousness of God in Christ Jesus! I stand confidently beside my Heavenly Father because Jesus paid the price for my sin!" (2 Corinthians 5:21).

One more thing!

I'm going to add a seventh piece of armor. What if there was one other thing that was attached to his belt? Could it be a little pouch that would hold some money? Of course, just like today? We always carry something in our pocket, stashed away somewhere safe, that we can use to trade for something else.

In our current culture, it's much easier (and now it's more effective) to wage economic war on a country by limiting or increasing trade. We don't need to send soldiers into a certain country to force the leadership to change its attitude. All we have to do is cut off their trade. So I believe, even though it's been this way forever, in today's time, we can add money to our tool belt as our armor.

So let's talk about money for a second from God's point of view. What does scripture say about trading commerce? He's very clear.

Give, and it will be given to you. A good measure, pressed down, shaken together, and running over, will be poured into your lap. For with the measure you use, it will be measured to you. (Luke 6:38).

If you perform a service or if you build a product, you will give it to someone, and they will give back to you more than it cost you to make or do. Commerce is all about giving. Our Heavenly Father is the master of commerce, believe it or not! So, how do we use this as a battle tool? Just like the other pieces, we can give under the leading of the Holy Spirit and change someone's life. We can administer them goodness and kindness to them by giving them something they do not deserve. How much has it blessed you and just melted your heart when your kids gave you something that was special to them?

Another way to use it as a tool is this: don't ever let anyone steal from you. If someone takes something that is yours and you can't get it back, give it to them. What they took will dissolve in their hands, but you will receive a Good Measure in return if you give it away. If you sell something for $50 that's worth $100, "give" the $50 to them. Don't let them take it from you. Sometimes I've done a job and, for instance, I told them I was going to charge $500, but it cost me $600 in time. It was my fault that I underestimated the job, so I can't get it back. What did I do? I "gave" them the hundred dollars. It's a "Win-Win"! They got an extra hundred dollars, but I sowed it as a seed and received 30, 60, or 100 times what I gave. So don't let anyone steal from you.

Put on Jesus' Clothes!

With Jesus' clothes on, your enemy sees God, not you. Don't let him see you; keep your armor on! This armor protects you and empowers you to face your enemy straight on and overcome him. Remember the first part of Ephesians 6? The battles we fight appear to be coming from people, but it's not the people we fight.

The Belt of Truth
The Breastplate of Righteousness
The Helmet of Salvation
Our Feet covered in Readiness
The Shield of Faith
The Sword of the Spirit

Questions:

What did you learn about building roofs today?
_____
_____

What is something you thought was true but Father showed you it was not true?
_____
_____

What was the truth or the scripture that you heard which led you to faith in Jesus when you got Born Again?
_____
_____

What part of the Armor are you most excited about putting to work?
_____
_____

What attacks have you been struggling with?
_____
_____

What part of the Armor will you use against your current struggle?
_____
_____

CHAPTER SIX

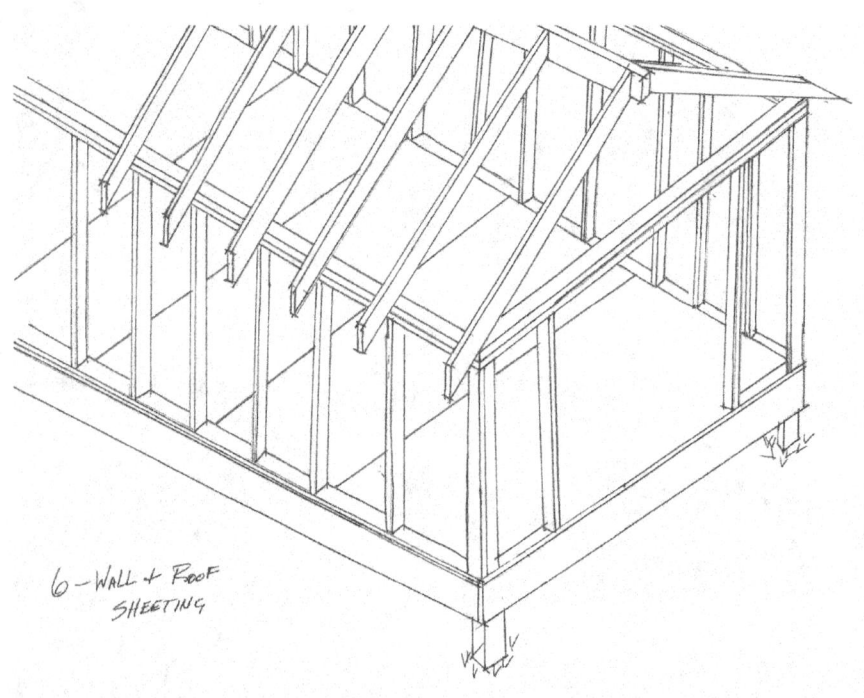

6 – WALL & ROOF SHEETING

The Prayer of a Father-Pastoring Your Life Well

Walls and Roofs, getting Covered!

In this session, we will install 7/16 OSB on the roof and T111 lap, smooth Smart Siding 4'x8' sheets on the side and end walls. This is the part of the shed that takes all the weather and must be made from the correct materials to withstand years of heat and cold, rain and snow, wind, and the scorching sun. There are lots of roofing materials we can choose from and each material requires its own procedure for installation. We can use metal sheets, which are more expensive but will last for many years and resist most weather conditions. We can use asphalt shingles, which are less expensive but can be damaged by hail and wind.

In this session, we will also be sheeting the walls with a wood composite called T-111 Smart Siding. It is water-resistant and carries a 30-year warranty, just like cement board does. The seams overlap on some versions. I like to caulk the seams to seal them from the water and air. We will be using ½" x 1 ¼" staples to secure the siding to the shed. Since the 4'x8' sheets are square, we will use them to square up our walls. Right now, the walls are very flimsy and rock back and forth easily. It's the siding that will give the shed walls their strength and make them very stable.

In our everyday life, we must build and establish our covering in order to successfully walk through the challenges that come every day. Jesus said that we should not worry about tomorrow; today is enough to work on.

"Therefore do not worry about tomorrow, for tomorrow will worry about itself. Each day has enough trouble of its own." (Matthew 6:34 NIV).

The truth is that we need to spend quality time with our Heavenly Father, using our faith for today. And that's enough! Don't worry about tomorrow. Planning for tomorrow is ok. That's something we will get instructions for today. But if we can master our internal world one day at a time, we can face the challenges of our external world with grace and power! If we can master today, we will be more than ready for tomorrow. Living under the shadow of the Roof is the key. This is living in Our Secret Place.

Looking back at where we've been, I believe Father has given us a Masterpiece of instruction. We've been shown who God is, who we are, and what Love is. Then He showed us, in Psalm 91, that if we trust in Him and center our lives around Him, He will bless us and rescue us from troubles. Lastly, He showed us how to wear His Clothes so we are protected from everyday attacks. We are learning how to put to work, and "Go Do", the Gospel in our workplace, at church, and most importantly in our home. To "apply" the Gospel to our everyday life and relationships. I think it's just a masterpiece of work. Today, Father is going to turn up the power!! He is going to show us how to put these things to work in our private lives as sons of God! A Son who knows His place with His Father. He is going to show us how to cover our wives and kids, keep ourselves in line with Him, and change lives around us every day. This is how we Be the Light in the world.

"Arise, shine; For your light has come! And the glory of the Lord is risen upon you." (Isaiah 60:1 NKJV).

During the time I was writing, editing, and administering this curriculum, I was dealing with this thought: "Is God really doing what I've been saying He would do?" I shared this message with the men the week before and then again with the elementary kids at church on Sunday. I felt like I was talking a lot about how God could, and would, do amazing things in our lives, but I was feeling like I was just not seeing it. Where was Father in my life?

Then on Monday morning—which is when I am writing this—I woke up asking Father about this situation. Suddenly, He began reminding me how He has been manifesting everything I have set my trust in Him for! What hadn't happened, I hadn't set my trust in Him for. I have been trusting Him for everyday stuff, and everyday stuff has been going very well. Bigger things have been happening, but oftentimes bigger things take some time, work, and progress we can't see. So we have to engage Patience, knowing He is working on stuff, and never give up.

This is when the devil loves to attack us with lots of little things and challenge our big plans with thoughts of impossibility. Then what we must do is stand firm in what we believe! Do what we were told last with professionalism and excellence, and keep moving forward even when everyone else would have given up and quit.

As we rise to the occasion with Jesus standing beside us, I guarantee that we will face this kind of opposition! Our enemy knows our every weakness, and he also knows how powerful we can be with Father by our side. So don't be surprised when past mistakes are brought up, weaknesses are exposed to the public, and when issues—which we usually don't have a problem with—occur and suddenly they are a big deal.

This is actually evidence that we are growing! We are putting pressure on our foundation because we are building on it! Every weakness and pain is being felt as the pressure forces it to the surface. Issues are rising up in our lives like never before, so turn to Father like never before! Lean on Him more heavily and Learn How to pray!

Years ago, I needed to find my Secret Place with God and live there! I was determined to find God! But I had a problem. I owned a restaurant at that time, and my routine consisted of getting up in time to take my girls to school, driving to the restaurant, working until 9 pm, driving 45 minutes home, taking a shower, and going to bed. 6 days a week, I did this for months without a break. But if I was going to have any peace, I was going to have to take a deeper step into my relationship with God.

He was still God, not so much Lord, and really not Father at that time.

My Prayer Story

When I was in college, I spent the summer in Dallas, Texas, and attended a church called "Church on the Rock". Dr Larry Lea was the pastor, and he taught extensively on prayer. He held prayer meetings Monday through Friday at 6 am. He also wrote several books on the subject of prayer. One was called, "Could You not Tarry One Hour". I read through that book but learned mostly how to pray, daily, from Dr Lea at his meetings and the early morning prayer. At the time I am writing this, he is still alive and preaching on prayer. You can also purchase his materials on Amazon.

I decided that, as I had done in college, I needed to get up an hour earlier than usual and pray. So I did, I got up and went right back to sleep. The next morning, I got up, went to the couch, and fell right to sleep. The next morning, I got up and stood on the edge of the shower curb. If I fell asleep, I would surely fall. Nope! That just hurt my feet. Then I talked with God about it.

I got the idea of taking a walk. So, the next day I got up and went to the couch to put my shoes on and fell asleep. I actually did that for three days in a row because I didn't want to go walking. Finally, the next day I got up and walked down my driveway, which was about ⅓ mile out and ⅓ mile back. I would love to tell you how glorious it was and how, like Moses, I saw God and talked with Him. But I didn't! Matter of fact, I got nothing! I trudged down the driveway, hating every step, dragging my feet, complaining, and pitifully trying to say the Lord's Prayer as I slowly and sleepily went along. Second day, I did the same thing with the same results.

Determination

At least I had determination. See, I heard this story told by Zig Ziglar about determination, and it goes like this:

There was a young man in his teens fishing with his grandpa while sitting on the edge of the dock overlooking a lake. The young man asked his very successful grandpa how he became so successful. After thinking about it for a minute, he took the fishing pole from his grandson and set it aside. Then he pushed his grandson into the water. When his grandson came up for air, he put his hand on his head and pushed him back under water and held him there. Then the young man began to fight his grandpa until finally he got free. Then his grandpa helped him back up on the dock.

The young man asked his grandpa why he did that, and his grandpa answered: **"When you want success as much as you want air, you'll fight just as hard to get it."**

I was a loser losing! I was a sad, mad, miserable orphan. And it was all my fault. But when I found out that there was a way out, I was all in. Nothing was going to stop me from finding my Secret Place with

God. Then the third day of my walking down the driveway came. I was a little more awake. Everything still hurt, and I was still tired, but I had stopped complaining. I walked ever so slowly down the driveway, turned around, and walked back. This time, I was about 100 feet from my house when I heard God for the first time in years. He said simply, "Good job."

I couldn't believe it, God talked to me. And I started telling Him everything that was bothering me. But all was silent. It was actually really good to get all that off my chest. The next day, I got up and hit the floor running. I was so excited about entering into my Secret Place with God.

After that and since then, I would usually hear nothing while I was walking, but at random and unexpected times, I would suddenly just know things! I would look up at the clouds in the sky and have visions, and God would explain them. Answers to prayers and requests began coming, and He began talking with me more and more. I even started keeping a journal of requests and was amazed that all of them got answered, and many times faster than it felt. At a pace I could handle, Father was healing my heart, and I started coming out of my sadness and anger at everyone and my bitter, negative attitude. It was such a relief, I had found Peace in The Secret Place of God!

As I walked and prayed the Lord's Prayer, things began to change, and Father began to teach me more about how to pray this way.

It's not a prayer, it's a prayer guide.

The purpose of this guide is to cover all the areas of your life. It's not for satisfying a requirement that God requests. It's for us, it's the guide we use to center our attitude, remind us of God's promises and who He is, hand over all our cares to Our Father, protect and intercede for our family and others, receive forgiveness, empower us to succeed, and give Him the praise which He deserves.

Disclaimer and warning!

Do not allow that orphan spirit to turn this into a checklist of things you must do to gain righteousness or something you do to get something you want. It's not even something you do to satisfy a need. This is about building and maintaining a relationship with your Heavenly Father from where you are. You are covering everything in your life with prayer. As you pray through this guide—given to us by Jesus—you will see that you are turning everything over to God. You must go through this slowly and with purpose, not just clicking off the requirements. If you allow this experience to go there, it will not work. It will not return anything to you, and it will become like a stillborn baby, dead on arrival, because there's no faith attached, no desire for intimacy with your Heavenly Father. It's a lot of work and requires determination, but if you deviate and allow your "father's choice" to change to a checklist that you proudly vomit up every day, what you depended on will crumble and fail.

So go through this slowly. If you don't get through all the parts, purposely continue during any "mind downtime" you have. If you don't finish, it's ok,

Do everything you do all day long WITH HIM, NOT WITHOUT HIM.

Then start fresh tomorrow. Remember, this is a journey with someone who loves you! He knows your strengths and weaknesses. Like a baby walking for the first time, our Heavenly Father loves walking us through growth! This path will be difficult, full of challenges, surprises, and failures. But it will also be full of rewards, inspiration, huge wins, peace in your heart, blessings, and awesome, God-inspired relationships!

Your destructive habits were not established in a day, and neither will your healthy habits.

Then, for various not-so-intelligent reasons, I quit praying like this for years. But a few months ago (At the time of this writing), I was asked to teach The Lord's Prayer to our kids at church. It was a refreshing reminder of the power of God available to us. To make it even more powerful, I had to condense it and simplify the prayer guide so 6, 7, and 8-year-old kids could put it to work at home and in their everyday life. Then I was reminded that I was actually teaching a message that Jesus taught! There is something very special about that. So, I started praying this way again, I haven't stopped, and I've seen results which I have never seen before! This is what we are going to learn today!

"**But** when you pray, go into your room, close the door, and pray to your Father, who is unseen. Then your Father, who sees what is done in secret, will reward you. And when you pray, do not keep on babbling like pagans, for they think they will be heard because of their many words. Do not be like them, for your Father knows what you need before you ask him. This, then, is how you should pray…" (Matthew 6:6-9 NIV).

The Our Father Prayer

There are seven parts in the outline which Jesus gave us in Matthew 6.

Part 1- Our Father in Heaven

"But seek first the kingdom of God and His righteousness, and all these things shall be added to you." (Matthew 6:33 NKJV).

In the days of Jesus, calling God your Father was not an acceptable thing to do! According to Matthew 26:63-66, the Pharisees believed it was blasphemous for someone to call God his Father. That was the final reason the High Priest found Jesus guilty enough for the death sentence, even though He really was the Son of God. It was Jesus who reintroduced "Lord God" to everyone as "Father" for the first time since Adam!

What a huge shock this must have been for His disciples! Just like it's a pretty big shock for most of us! Thinking logically about this, Jesus followed the Law of Moses strictly. He lived His life blameless and without sin; therefore, we could argue that He could claim the title, "Son of God"! But can we claim that same title? Yes! Jesus did everything He did so we could be Sons of God too! Adopted into His family with the Creator of All Things as Our Father! Pretty awesome deal for us! But we must choose!

"For you are all sons of God through faith in Christ Jesus." (Galatians 3:26 NKJV).

Paul is telling us that we need to choose to be Sons of our Heavenly Father. This is something we must do every day, all day long. So we start our time in the Secret Place, acknowledging and choosing

THE Heavenly Father as OUR Heavenly Father.

Take a moment and "choose" Him as your Father. Just be still in yourself. Direct your attention away from everything else and to your Heavenly Father as if He is physically sitting right here beside you. Simply acknowledge His presence with you. Declare that you will choose Him all day today, by faith, with every decision you make.

I have learned that, as our heart has layers of depth, we will be given the opportunity to choose Him at deeper and deeper levels. We should learn to keep The Father as Our Father and not choose another. The Holy Spirit is there, and He will help us and remind us if we acknowledge Him or not.

So why do we have to choose? Because we have the choice to make someone else or something else, our father.

Jesus said to them, "If God were your Father, you would love Me, for I proceeded forth and came from God; nor have I come of Myself, but He sent Me. Why do you not understand my speech? Because you are not able to listen to My word. You are of your father the devil, and the desires of your father you want to do. He was a murderer from the beginning, and does not stand in the truth, because there is no truth in him. When he speaks a lie, he speaks from his own resources, for he is a liar and the father of it." (John 8:42-44 NKJV).

So, because we have a choice, every day we set our mind and heart to choose The Father as Our Father and no other. It's because of Him, with Him, for Him, and through Him we make every decision. We will not fall back on our old ways of doing things—seeking created things to satisfy our lust and soothe the pain in our hearts.

Sometimes the truth appears to be such a logical and obvious choice that we cannot see the value in it. So, to look at the negative side, when we see someone who has obviously made some wrong decisions and is now facing the consequences, we can conclude that they simply chose the wrong father. We can see in John 8 that Jesus identified the Father whom the priests chose. He is a liar and the father of lies, a murderer, and since they chose him, they want to do what he does.

So the choice is ours. Who will we choose? The murdering father of lies who wants to destroy us and everyone we love? Or the Father of all Creation who loves us, protects us, helps us, feeds us, heals us, tells us the truth, gives us life, and gave His life for us? I choose the Father of Creation! How about you?

Therefore, we declare: Father! Today you are my Father, and there is no other! I will not choose the father of lies, I will choose You all day today. I will not allow anything or anyone else to take Your place as Father in my life today. Thank You for being My Heavenly Father today.

Part 2– Holy is Your Name

Next, we recognize who God is. Through history, when Father did something significant, either He gave Himself a name or a person gave Him a name that defined a characteristic of who He is because of what He did.

Jehovah Mec'hadish— God my Sanctification. He is the One who forgives and cleanses us. This name was given by God to Moses to establish that He is the One who sanctifies us or sets us apart, cleansing us from the ways of the world. He establishes boundaries to keep us from harm.

This name was introduced in the book of Exodus.

Speak also to the children of Israel, saying: "Surely My Sabbaths you shall keep, for it is a sign between Me and you throughout your generations, that you may know that *I am the Lord who sanctifies you*." (Exodus 31:13 NKJV).

Jehovah Tsidkenu— God my Righteousness. I have been made the Righteousness of God in Christ, and I have right standing with God through what Jesus did on the cross for me. As we learned with the Breastplate of Righteousness, I have the right to stand next to God. He is my Righteousness.

This name was introduced in the book of Jeremiah.

"For the time is coming," says the Lord, "when I will raise up a righteous descendant from King David's line. He will be a King who rules with wisdom. He will do what is just and right throughout the land. And this will be his name: '*The Lord Is Our Righteousness*.' In that day Judah will be saved, and Israel will live in safety." (Jeremiah 23:5-6 NLT).

Jehovah Shalom— God is my Peace. Peace in the Hebrew language refers to completeness, wholeness, nothing missing, and all together. My Heavenly Father completes me, makes me whole, and completes everything I have influence over. He is the Peace in my heart, Peace in my home, Peace at work, and everywhere I go. He is the Peace Who never leaves me.

The first use of Jehovah Shalom was in the book of Judges.

When Gideon realized that it was the angel of the Lord, he exclaimed, "Alas, Sovereign Lord! I have seen the angel of the Lord face to face!" But the Lord said to him, "Peace! Do not be afraid. You are not going to die." So Gideon built an altar to the Lord there and called it *The Lord Is Peace*. To this day it stands in Ophrah of the Abiezrites." (Judges 6:22-24 NIV).

Jehovah Rapha— He is my Healer. Jesus' body was beaten so my body could be healed and restored.

"But He was wounded for our transgressions, He was bruised for our iniquities; The chastisement for our peace was upon Him, And by His stripes we are healed." (Isaiah 53:5 NKJV).

Father described Himself as a Healer for the first time in Exodus.

He said, "If you listen carefully to the Lord your God and do what is right in his eyes, if you pay attention to his commands and keep all his decrees, I will not bring on you any of the diseases I brought on the Egyptians, for *I am the Lord, who heals you.*" (Exodus 15:26 NIV).

Jehovah Jireh— He is my Provider. It was Abraham who first called God "Provider" because He provided a ram for a sacrifice in the place of his son Issac.

So Abraham called that place The Lord Will Provide. And to this day it is said, "On the mountain of the *Lord it will be provided*." (Genesis 22:14 NIV).

Jehovah Nissi— He is my Banner. He goes before me and fights my battles.

"You prepare a table before me in the presence of my enemies. You anoint my head with oil; my cup overflows." (Psalms 23:5 NIV).

The first time God was called "My Banner" was when Joshua was fighting the Amalekites. Moses was watching from a distance, and when he held up his hands, the Israelites would win the battle. When he dropped his hands, because he was tired, they would lose. So like a banner waving in the air, our Father fights our battles.

"Moses built an altar and called it *The Lord is my Banner."* (Exodus 17:15 NIV).

Jehovah Rohi—He is my Shepherd. He guides and leads me and takes care of me everywhere I go.

King David first called God his Shepherd in Psalm 23.

"*The Lord is my shepherd*, I lack nothing." (Psalms 23:1 NIV).

We establish these truths of Who God is by declaring by faith the names He has been called in the past. Who has Father been to you? Take some time here to praise Him, thank Him, and remind yourself of the things He has done for you. Who has He been in your life? Declare these things also!

This is so very important! Exhaust your knowledge of God. When you do, your spiritual ears will open to hear His Voice, and if you listen, you will hear Him reveal something about Himself that you didn't know before. This is vitally important for us to continue effectively.

Don't go through this prayer so fast. Be sensitive to the Holy Spirit as you progress through the steps. If you get stuck here, just remain thankful all day. It's ok. This is not the magic combination to wealth and success. It is the combination of a relationship like you have never had before. So take your time and let every part settle in your spirit. Let your faith attach itself to every truth and then move on.

Know that it is from Your Heavenly Father, from whom ALL Blessings flow.

"All these blessings will come on you and accompany you if you obey the Lord your God…" (Deuteronomy 28:2 NIV).

Choose this Guy—who does all these things—to be your Father and make Him your source for all you need, today! Re-establish Father every day in your heart and mind. This choice we make is the foundation for what is next!

Part 3 Your kingdom come, Your will be done here on earth as it is in heaven.

It is very important for us to freshly establish—in our heart—who God is before we move on to the rest of the prayer. Remember, Father's first priority in everything is to establish a deeper relationship with Him. If we don't remember and value that as much as He does, we will get disappointed when our prayers don't get answered.

Don't let yourself get discouraged and disappointed. Turn your heart towards Him (when your prayers don't seem to manifest) and seek Him and find rest in the fact that maybe this thing you are asking for is not as important as you thought and maybe you need to learn something else more important.

Sometimes, at this point, I get so caught up in the awe of who He is that I just want to stop there and be thankful. And there is nothing wrong with that. It's perfectly ok to simply stay in this posture of being thankful and absorbing who He is deeper into our hearts. This purifies our hearts and builds our faith. It prepares our faith for the declarations ahead.

Now that we have chosen Him and established in our hearts who He is toward us, we can believe that His Kingdom and His will for us is the best possible scenario for our life!

In this part, we make a declaration of faith. The enemy really likes to get me to stop here and not do this. He is in deep trouble when I get through this part! We always need to ask first, but after asking, we need to make a declaration of faith. So I always make a faith declaration since I have already asked for these things.

In English, it sounds somewhat passive to say, "Your kingdom come, Your will be done," but I have been told that in the Greek, it is very declarative, forceful, and strong. Like we are to force Father's perfect will to be done in our lives. Does that sound weird? It's not. This is what Father wants for us: His perfect will to be done in our lives! It can't get any better than that!

Therefore, I declare over myself, my wife, and my kids: Father, I declare: "Your kingdom will be established in our hearts and in our minds today. I declare that Your perfect will is being done in our lives today. No weapon formed against us shall prosper, and no matter what I see, Your perfect will is being done in our lives today." Then I declare this for the rest of my family and anyone else special that comes to mind. I declare this over every pastor, teacher, and anyone who administers the Gospel around the world, over every government official, over every born-again believer in the world. I also declare this over you, every day. For those of you who hear the message Father has given us for this day and time. Then I will pause and wait to hear from the Holy Spirit for anyone else I need to declare this over. I can't think of a more powerful way to intercede for someone.

Then, when my kids, my wife or anyone else does something I don't agree with, or I feel afraid that they might be in trouble or sick, I remind myself that I have already put them in His hands and His Perfect Will, will be done in their life, **TODAY**, somehow, some way because I have declared it so, by faith!

Part 4– Give us this day our daily bread.

"Then Jesus declared, "I am the bread of life. Whoever comes to me will never go hungry, and whoever believes in me will never be thirsty." (John 6:35 NIV).

Remember the story of the seven women who asked to marry the one man, only for His name in the book of Isaiah 4:1? This is the "food" they rejected from their husband. The Bread of Life—Jesus! But we want His Food! We received His food and refused to provide our own food to eat today!

God gave manna to the millions of Israelites in the desert for 40 years. Daily, he provided bread! There were some rules for collecting and storing the bread. But they prepared it in all

kinds of ways. Then, when Jesus came, the people asked Him to give them bread every day like Moses did.

"Jesus said to them, "Very truly I tell you, it is not Moses who has given you the bread from heaven, but it is my Father who gives you the true bread from heaven. For the bread of God is the bread that comes down from heaven and gives life to the world." "Sir," they said, "always give us this bread." Then Jesus declared, "I am the bread of life. Whoever comes to me will never go hungry, and whoever believes in me will never be thirsty." (John 6:32-35 NIV).

"Let them shout for joy and be glad, who favor my righteous cause; And let them say continually, 'Let the Lord be magnified, Who has pleasure in the prosperity of His servant." (Psalms 35:27 NKJV).

It gives your Heavenly Father Joy to see you prosper! This is the prayer from the heart of a son! A son should never choose to worry about having enough because he knows his Heavenly Father has provided seed to the farmer and bread for those who have the right to stand next to him. And we have that right by faith in what Jesus did for us on the cross!

"For as the rain comes down, and the snow from heaven, And do not return there, But water the earth, And make it bring forth and bud, That it may give seed to the sower And bread to the eater, So shall My word be that goes forth from My mouth; It shall not return to Me void, But it shall accomplish what I please, And it shall prosper in the thing for which I sent it." (Isaiah 55:10-11 NKJV).

We declare: Father, today I receive Jesus as my Bread of Life. I will eat from Your table today, and I refuse to try to provide for myself. I will pick up every piece of bread you lay out for me today ,and I will be responsible for using it and distributing it as you command. I receive financial bread, mental kinds of bread, spiritual bread, and relationship kinds of bread. Everything you have for me. I will receive every provision you have for every area of my life. I will gladly and thankfully return to You the 10%

You ask for, and You said You will open the windows of Heaven and pour out a Blessing on m   which I will not be able to contain. I will joyfully give as You ask so I may be a Blessing and a witness of Your Love and generosity to others. I will be thankful for everything, all the time. I will remember that everything good comes from You, and I don't need to be worried about today or tomorrow because You are providing to me everything as I can receive it!

I am a tither. I will be responsible with everything You give me according to Malachi.

"Bring all the tithes into the storehouse so there will be enough food in my Temple. If you do," says the Lord of Heaven's Armies, "I will open the windows of heaven for you. I will pour out a blessing so great you won't have enough room to take it in! Try it! Put me to the test!" (Malachi 3:10 NLT).

Thank you for providing me with everything I need today, and more!

Part 5– Forgive us our sins as we forgive those who sin against us.

"If we confess our sins, He is faithful and just to forgive us our sins and to cleanse us from all unrighteousness." (I John 1:9 NKJV).

"Make allowance for each other's faults, and forgive anyone who offends you. Remember, the Lord forgave you, so you must forgive others." (Colossians 3:13 NLT).

God gave us the Gift of Forgiveness when we made Jesus the Lord of our lives and confessed our sins to Him. Father forgave us of all sin through the death and resurrection of Jesus—the act of the cross! It was a gift that we could not pay enough for. It's a gift we keep. But then, when someone offends us or hurts us, we can give them this

Gift of Forgiveness, which we were given. When we give the Gift of Forgiveness, we don't ever go without. Just as soon as we give Forgiveness, the Gift reappears in our hearts. We can't ever give it away so much that we don't have any.

This part of the prayer is like a sensor that warns us that we need forgiveness. If it's difficult for us to forgive, we need forgiveness! We cannot give the Gift of Forgiveness if we don't have it! So this sensor warning tells us that we need to turn to our Father and ask what we have done wrong that we need to receive forgiveness for. And receive it! Now we will have the capacity to forgive again.

I thank my Heavenly Father for coming here and suffering and dying for me and paying the price for my sin! Ok. This just blesses me so much what I'm about to say:

My Heavenly Father is the only God who bleeds!
He's the only one who hurts for me. He's the only one who would and could die and raise Himself back to life for only one reason—to create a special place for me, right beside Him! That is just absolutely amazing! So I thank Him for forgiving me! For all the big things I'm already forgiven for and for all the little things I know of and don't know of. Because of this, sin is not an issue between me and God. He forgave my sin. So receive the Gift!

"So if you are presenting a sacrifice at the altar in the Temple and you suddenly remember that someone has something against you, leave your sacrifice there at the altar. Go and be reconciled to that person. Then come and offer your sacrifice to God." (Matthew 5:23-24 NLT).

"For God so loved the world that he gave his one and only Son, that whoever believes in him shall not perish but have eternal life." (John 3:16 NIV).

We wouldn't even know what love was if Father hadn't shown us first.

"We love because he first loved us." (1 John 4:19 NIV).

And love forgives! (1 Corinthians 13) So we cannot forgive others if we haven't been forgiven. You can't give a gift you don't already have! But when you do have it, you can and want to give it away as freely as you got it.

We need to check our hearts to see if there is anything we need to confess and receive forgiveness for.

Father, I receive Your Gift of forgiveness and Love for me today. I will give the gift of forgiveness and your Love to anyone in need. I choose to forgive those who have hurt me or offended me in any way. Examine my heart and reveal to me anyone I need to forgive, and I will. Reveal to me anything I need forgiveness for. Thank you for forgiving me today, and I declare that I will forgive today.

Part 6– Lead us not into temptation, but deliver us from evil.

"Instead, clothe yourself with the presence of the Lord Jesus Christ. And don't let yourself think about ways to indulge your evil desires." (Romans 13:14 NLT).

"Put on the full armor of God, so that you can take your stand against the devil's schemes." (Ephesians 6:10-11 NIV).

This is the part where we put on Our Father's clothes, His Armor.

Again, remember the revelation Father gave us about the seven women who asked to marry the one man only for his name in Isaiah 4:1? They said they would clothe themselves. They rejected His clothes. This is where we accept only our Father's Clothes. His Armor. His Robe of Righteousness!

This is how Father deals with us! After all, we are His SONS!

This was covered in much-deserved detail in session 5. We need Father's Armor because the biggest challenges we face today and every day are not our lack of finances or healing for our body, but the people we must contend with. We are the example of our Father, we are the light of the world, so how we deal with people is the biggest responsibility we have and, as a result, the biggest battle we face. Our enemy will constantly attempt to convince us to act unlike our Father. So let's go through it.

The Belt of Truth
The Breastplate of Righteousness.
My feet fitted with readiness to share the Gospel of Peace.
I take up the Shield of Faith and extinguish all the flaming arrows of the evil one.
Put on the Helmet of Salvation!
Take up the Sword of the Spirit!

Part 7– For Yours is the Glory and power and dominion forever!

Praise the Lord!
Yes, give praise, O servants of the Lord.
Praise the name of the Lord!
Blessed be the name of the Lord now and forever.
Everywhere—from east to west— praise the name of the Lord.
For the Lord is high above the nations; his glory is higher than the heavens.
Who can be compared with the Lord our God, who is enthroned on high?
He stoops to look down on heaven and on earth.
He lifts the poor from the dust and the needy from the garbage dump.
He sets them among princes, even the princes of his own people!
He gives the childless woman a family, making her a happy mother.
Praise the Lord!
(Psalms 113:1-9 NLT).

This last part of the prayer is the icing on the cake! When you commune with your Heavenly Father this way, amazing things will begin to happen. We thank Him for who He is and what He is going to do. But more than that, we declare and choose in advance to give Him all the Glory when others praise us for what He has done through us. Because it wasn't really us doing it, was it? Lots of times I will say,

"If it was good, it was God. If it was all messed up, it was me."

Sometimes people are praised for doing a good job at something, and they falsely say, "Oh, it was all God!" And it really wasn't that good. So to keep from embarrassing yourself, just say "Thank you". Then give your Father the credit for empowering you to do what you couldn't have done by yourself. This is how we give our Father the Glory for what He has done without giving Him the credit for the not-so-great things we did.

We need to show others that they can do what we have done (and better) if they choose the same Father that we have chosen.

So Jesus said, "When you have lifted up the Son of Man on the cross, then you will understand that I am He. I do nothing on my own but say only what the Father taught me. And the One who sent Me is with Me—He has not deserted Me. For I always do what pleases Him." (John 8:28-29 NLT).

Father! I thank You for everything You are doing in my life today! All day today, I give You all the Glory and Praise because You have all the Power and Dominion over everything! You are the Almighty! And you are my Father! I give you all the Glory all the time with everyone, and I take none of Your Glory for myself. I will be thankful today and not complain about anything. I have trusted in You for the best for myself and others, and I thank You for that honor and privilege today! Thank You! Amen!

Conclusion

Celebrate! You are on the track of success, peace, and a relationship that cannot be matched by anyone or anything! Following this guide that Jesus gave us will, little by little and at your own pace, open your heart to a loving Father whom you did not know. You may not be able to open up to other men or someone else, but you can open up to your Heavenly Father about anything. This is one key to true Peace. Being transparent is a major issue we all have, but we can open up to Father because He will not hurt us, shame us, or degrade us.

Father desires to redeem us, help us, uplift us, and empower us until we can stand next to Him, confidently wielding His power and Love as He holds our hand and walks us through every step.

Questions:

What was the cool thing you learned about building today?
_____
_____

How do you feel about narrowing down your faith to the events of today instead of trying to worry about the future?
_____
_____

What was your favorite verse today?
_____
_____

Where can you apply the 3rd part of the prayer: Your Kingdom come, Your will be done?
_____
_____

Make your choice in advance. When will you make time to pray tomorrow?
_____
_____

CHAPTER SEVEN

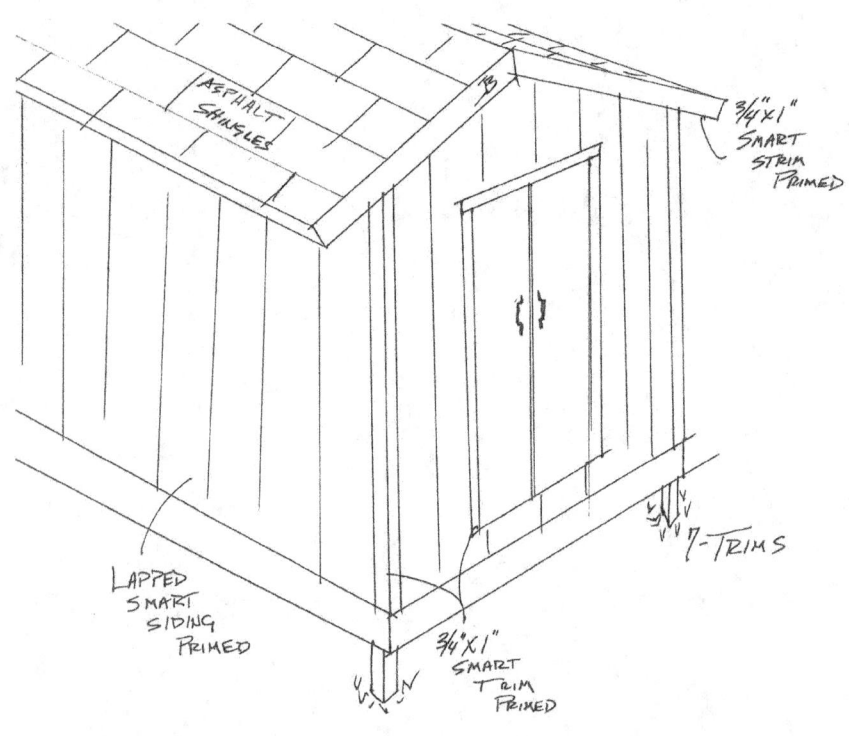

The Final Touches! This is More Important Than That!

Today, we will be trimming out the shed. The purpose of trim is to cover seams. Clean up corners and seal edges so water doesn't leak in. Trim Carpentry requires quite a bit more exact cutting than framing and siding require. The process is slower, but also enjoyable because when we are done, everything is going to look really good!

This is more important than that.
I have been dealing with getting out of bed and spending time with Father. Every morning—for years now—He has been waking me up at various times between 3 am and 6 am so I will get up and spend some time with Him. It has been a battle to actually get up, though. Instead of welcoming the ever-so-gentle request, I have been talking myself into believing that I am awake and I am thankful and I'm here, but I just don't want to move. So I lay awake, not able to really go back to sleep, fighting the persistent request until finally I went back to slee,p only to wake up disappointed in myself again.

One morning, again, I lay awake in my bed, not getting up but talking with my Father. Then I did get up, and because it was late, I got dressed and went to work. On the way, He was suggesting that I stop and spend just a few minutes with Him quietly. I went to Lowe's with the intention to stop, but I didn't. I went inside, bought what I needed, got in my truck, and drove off, still not stopping. Then again, the request came to pause and rest in Him, but I kept driving to the job, thinking I would stop when I got there. When I arrived, I was thinking about all the things I needed to do and how far behind I was. So I got out of my truck and began unloading tools.

Then I heard this,

"This is more important than that."

And I was reminded (See, I already knew this! I just wasn't following the wisdom I had gotten!) that spending 5 minutes with My Heavenly Father—the One who created the universe with a word—was more important than the 5 minutes I was going to spend working. My logic was saying that my work was more important. He was saying that my time with Him was more important.

Then again, He said, "You know you can easily waste 5 minutes and even an hour. You can work hard all day and get nothing done. You can get frustrated, hurt, and disappointed, and in the process of pushing through the pain, damage your heart. Both of them! Your physical heart, by the stress, and your spiritual heart by rebellion and fear. Or you can spend 5 minutes with me and you can get two days of work done in one day without all the pain."

So I stopped, turned around, and got back into my truck, saying to myself,

"This is more important than that."

 Sure enough, Father had something important He wanted to download to me. And after about 5 minutes, when we were done, I went to work and my day went so much better than the days previous.

Sometimes (ok, a lot of times, maybe most of the time) I think we forget who we are dealing with. Our Heavenly Father is not an idea, a power, or a force. He is a person whom we were made like!! Believing in Him more doesn't make Him more powerful; He is already all-powerful!

Believing in Him more makes us more powerful!

Others can argue that what they believe is more powerful than what I believe. The truth is that there is no contest! It doesn't matter if everyone believes in Jesus or no one believes in Him. He is still the Creator of all things with no beginning and no end! It doesn't matter what I believe about Him or what someone else believes about Him; He is still the Creator of all things! He does not change!

And this is the battle we fight every day! If the devil can get us to think that God, Jesus, is someone who we can make bigger or smaller with our imagination, then he can limit our positive influence. And influence is our greatest asset! It is also our second most important priority in life. The first priority in life is simply to be His Son!

This is more important than that!

Sonship is more important than anything else.

"What do I do when I spend time with God?"

First— I change my image of God from "God" to "Loving Father" whose first priority is to fellowship, talk with, work with ,and to impart some wisdom to me!

Second—I believe and understand that He knows me better than I know myself! He wants the best for me always! And that helps me know Him is His first priority.

Third— The Word, talking with Father, listening, and Praise is a great way to start. (I got this message when I sat down to spend 5 minutes with My Father.) I always begin by being quiet and waiting for instructions. If I don't get anything, within about 30 seconds, I go to my Bible and start reading—where I left off—because I have a reading plan. Then I am sensitive to where I am led next. Sometimes I pray the Lord's Prayer. Sometimes I play a worship song that comes to mind. But I always finish telling My Father how thankful I am for Him and His Word. Then, when I get up, I choose to be determined to acknowledge Father's presence with me all day. I do nothing without Him, and I do everything with Him. This is how we should start our day, live our day, and end our day.

So this is my challenge! We can waste 5 minutes very easily. We can waste an hour easily. We can even waste a whole day! But if that's so easy, why can't we set an alarm and spend 5 minutes with Our Father? We can!

I taught this at church last Sunday to my Kindergartner through 2nd-grade class. I challenged them to spend 5 minutes with God. The next day, I ran into one of the dads. He said that his two kids asked him to help them set a timer and spend 5 minutes with Jesus, so they did! He said that 15 minutes later, they were still talking to Jesus! Finally, he told them that they can't stay up all night! They needed to go to bed! Wow! I can't wait to hear what happened in their life this week!

So let's just stop and be quiet for 5 minutes and see what Father does!

What did Your Heavenly Father say to you?

_____

_____

The Orphan Heart

We have talked a bit about Sonship and the issues of the orphan heart that we face. Today, we will dive deeper into that subject.

There are so many examples of men and women in the Bible who made their choices from the heart of a Son and from the heart of an orphan. This is a huge battle that we all fight every single day. Because of that, it is very important for us to understand what we are fighting for and how to deal with it all. If the devil can keep us from knowing who we are, or get us to forget who we are, then he has us defeating ourselves, and he doesn't have to do anything else. This is why we already established the foundation of who we were created to be and who we can be in Christ Jesus. But that orphan likes to sneak around and con us into changing what we believe about ourselves because he knows that what we believe about ourselves is what carves out our character.

"For as he thinks in his heart, so is he." (Proverbs 23:7 NKJV).

Notice King Solomon did not say that a man is as he thinks in his mind! No, a man is as he believes in his heart. God didn't waste any time establishing this in Adam's heart. The first thing He did was have him name the animals.

Adam co-created with God!

Today, our understanding of the use of names is very different from God's. We use a name to label someone so we can differentiate between two people. God uses names to assign character and establish a future. Remember how Jesus called Simon, Peter, the Rock, or James and John, the Sons of Thunder? Father has always established/created character with a name. And this is what God did with Adam right away.

According to Biblehub.com, this act of naming the animals was not like naming your cat, Fluffy or your dog, Fido. It was to establish the character of the animals. So when God brought a lion to Adam, he actually decided its character and its role on the earth. He was co-creating with God! Wow! Amazing!

Biblehub.com

In ancient Hebrew culture, the act of calling or naming was significant. Names were often given with the hope of reflecting character or destiny. Proclamations were important in communal and religious settings, where messages from God or leaders were declared to the people. Reading aloud was a common practice, especially in the context of teaching and preserving oral traditions.

Father was establishing the definition of identity in Adam's heart. And it worked! Adam learned that He was created by and like God! He was God's creative "Helper"! We know this because the next statement is that Adam couldn't find a helper suitable for him. Adam saw that he was God's helper, so he needed a helper too. Then God created Eve—his helper!

Abram needed a "Name" change!

Father told Abram that he needed to leave his home and that he would be blessed. So Abram left his family and traveled. And God blessed him, and he became very rich. Abram was grateful but told God that everything he owned would be passed to his servant because Sarai was barren and they couldn't have any kids. But God took Abram outside and showed him the stars in the sky and told him that he would have a multitude of children. But for years, Abram still didn't have any kids. So Sarai got an idea and Abram went along with it. They were going to help God out with this Kid problem. She gave him her maid,

Hagar, to be his wife. And she gave birth to a son, Ishmael. But God told Hagar that Ishmael would become a great nation, but would be violent, fighting everyone, and everyone fighting him. (This is true to this day.) Mr. Abram was 86 years old at the time.

Then, when Abram was 99 years old, God spoke to him again. God told Abram to walk before Him blameless and that He wanted to make a covenant with him. Abram knew he had messed up, so he fell at Father's feet. See, in those days, a covenant was a serious thing. Someone always richer and powerful would make a covenant or a contract with someone less rich and powerful. This contract/covenant benefited both parties and made the lesser equal with the greater. So Abram was very humbled by this request God was making. His command to be blameless was not just a request but a creative command. God was about to do what Adam did with the animals. He was going to "name" him! And God changed his name from Abram—exalted father— to Abraham—father of many nations! God also changed Sarai's name to Sarah, which means Mother of many nations. God added the "ha" to Abram. "Ha" is "God" in Hebrew.

Remember the name YHWH? It's unpronounceable. It's the sound of a breath in and out. "Ha" is the last part of YHWH, which is the breath out. God inserted Himself into who Abram and Sarai were and created a new image inside their heart. Now Abraham believed that not only could he prosper in everything he put his hands to, but he also believed he could be a dad too!! And at 100 years old, he was a Dad!!

Names change how we see ourselves on the inside. But what we see every day—the environment we are in—has molded us into who we are. This is also a scientifically and socially proven fact. In recent history, we have built brand new apartment buildings, furnished them, and moved homeless people into them. We would think that they would be grateful and take really good care of the property because it was given to them, right? No! They trashed the place until it was unlivable. Why? Because poverty was in their heart, and what is in a person's heart, they will create in their environment.

Am I a slave or a free man?

There is a saying, "It's easy to get a man out of jail but difficult to get the jail out of a man." Look at the children of Israel. They were slaves in Egypt for 400 years. God had to rescue Moses from slavery and raise him in the palace of Pharaoh as royalty in order to create a free man inside his heart. And Moses freed the Israelites from slavery because he could "see" a free Israel in his heart.

Joseph was a leader in his family as a boy and a free man in his heart. So when he was sold into slavery in Potiphar's house, what did he do? He created his freedom where he lived, resulting in being promoted to the level just under his master. Then, when he was put into jail, he didn't just stay a prisoner; he created his freedom inside the jail, and before long, he was managing the jail. Even though it was still a jail, he asked one of the new prisoners why he was so sad. The prisoner had a dream that was really bothering him. But look at that! Joseph had created such a comfortable JAIL that it was unusual if a prisoner was sad! Wow! What a transformation Joseph made in prison!

What does your heart look like?

What does your home look like? What does your truck or car look like? What does your closet look like? What does your life look like? It's a reflection of areas in your heart. I enjoy my home. It's not really a 100% reflection of my heart; it's more of a reflection of Claudia's heart. It's not perfect and it needs some repairs (That's my fault!) ,but it's neat and clean and in some kind of order. Although if you go out to my barn, it's a whole other story! My barn is a mess! Why? Because in my heart, I'm a mess in a certain area! It really does reflect how I feel inside sometimes.

I didn't use to be this way. I have always been super organized, and I always knew where everything was. As a kid, I always kept my dad's barn organized and clean. I made places for all his stuff, and I never let the floor get dirty. When I ran a convenience store, everything had its place and everything was always clean. My office was organized, and I even stayed up until 3 am to wax the floors twice a year. I always knew how much food I had on hand and how much I needed to buy every week. I had my money budgeted down to the dollar. After that, every job I ever got, they would have me organize everything first. It's just how I was. Then I got burned in one business, which I owned, and had to shut it down. I became angry at people in general and as I became more bitter, the clutter and disorganization in my heart overwhelmed me.

As I am writing this today, I am struggling with the mess in my heart. But God is working. See, out of that mess, I have created many beautiful things too. I have two very organized, neat, beautiful, and useful pieces of furniture which I built in my barn. Out of the mess in my truck, I build, remodel, and repair things all day long. Right now, it's keeping me humble. I know I have things that aren't right and need to change, but I also know that my Father is bigger than my mess. I believe Father wants you to see that when you see me, you'll see someone really not perfect, sometimes a mess, but out of that mess, Father can make really cool stuff! And He can do the same thing in your heart, too! You are not too far gone.

"Oh, but there's a sin that's unforgivable!", you might say, "What if I have committed that sin?" That sin is the sin of an unrepentant heart. If you don't want God as your Father, He doesn't have to be. You can choose anyone you want. But since He is the Truth, you will be buying into a lie. It's your choice. It's not that you can't go back to Him; you don't want to go back to Him. How can you be redeemed and forgiven if you don't want it? You can't. But you can be redeemed if you want it!

We are not the sum total of our actions.

So this is the devil's master plan: change what you believe about yourself in your heart. He is always trying to attach our identity to our sin and our actions. God is always trying to disconnect our identity from our actions. We are not the total of our actions. We are a Child of God because that's how He created us! People trust us, or do not trust us, based on our actions. So our actions are a vital ingredient to our influence. When we ask Father to fix some of these problems, many times He will work on our hearts first because that is where the problem really lies.

Have you ever had a time when you felt like you had it all together, but stuff didn't come together? Or you were going to get serious about seeking God, and you really set everything aside to follow after God with everything you are and maybe you fasted for days, read your Bible all the way through, or prayed every day for weeks needing a breakthrough, and just didn't get it? Or you did that once and got your breakthrough but this time it didn't come? Yup! That has happened to me, too!

I know a guy who was struggling in his business. He began seeking God for direction and wisdom for his business and his career. After weeks of no results and no answers, he was frustrated and disappointed, so he began asking God why He was not answering. Father's response was,

"I am working on growing a man, not a business."

What a profound and wise answer! Many time,s we need maturity more than we need the Blessing we want. The image inside needs to change in order to support the outside change we are asking for.

The truth is that we are a new creation of God, through the death and resurrection of Jesus, for the forgiveness of sin and redemption of our souls.

We are a prototype!

Nothing has ever been done like us before. We're the first people who can live in heaven and on earth at the same time. We bring heaven to earth! This is the image we need to nurture in our hearts. This is why we must believe that we are Sons of God and not orphans! The first attack on that belief comes when we are given the choice to be offended.

Warning sign #1– Offense

If you feel offended by something someone said or did, you are looking through the open door to a path that will damage your heart, alienate it from others, make you vulnerable to attack ,and lead you away from your Heavenly Father. In Genesis 3:4, the serpent manipulated Eve, knowing that Adam and Eve's greatest desire was to be like God. He lied to Eve saying that God was trying to prevent them from being like Him because He told them not to eat of the Tree of the Knowledge of Good and Evil. This was just not true! He was trying to change what Eve believed about herself! In the first chapter of Genesis, we see that God made man in His own image and likeness (Genesis 1:26). Adam and Eve were already like God! They just needed to grow in knowledge, but only after receiving Life first! Think about it.

The knowledge of good and evil is what scares the unbeliever to death! Literally! They run from evil and are skeptical of anything good, especially things that are unbelievably good, like our Heavenly Father. But for those of us who are born again, the knowledge of Good, with the guidance of the Holy Spirit, increases our faith and trust in our Heavenly Father. Knowledge of evil, again with the help of the Holy Spirit, helps us make the choice to avoid evil. This was Father's perfect design!

It's kind of like eating fruit, cheese, and nuts. When you chew it all up, you end up with a new flavor that is better than all three separately. So watch out for offense! When it comes, do not run through that door! Run to your Heavenly Father and receive His Life, His Love, His Wisdom, and His instruction.

This instruction is vital to follow. For example, If a lady gets "offended" by her husband because he is physically abusive to her or her kids, the Wisdom she should use is to get out and seek some help. I am not talking about abusive and dangerous situations. You are responsible for your own actions, so seek some help if you're not sure what to do. If at work, your boss is rude to you, don't allow offense to come into your heart. Run to Your Father and ask Him what to do. He might tell you to stay there and give you grace with your boss because He wants to change his life with your example. But he might also tell you to quit that job and find a new one.

Always, every day, seek to live in the Perfect Will of your Heavenly Father. We start our day with that declaration because today He might be telling you to stay, and tomorrow He might tell you to leave! King Solomon said that there is a time for everything under the sun. (Ecclesiastes 3:1) In other words, don't get offended and leave your Shepherd! Stay with Him because He is the only one who knows when to stay and when to go. The idea is not to follow what **you** think is best for **you** at the time in **your** own opinion; the idea is to follow **His** will for you, and it may change at any moment.

As a parent, to keep our kids from being offended by things we do and decisions we make, we must practice apologizing for every offense when we are wrong. Sometimes we may do something that hurts our kids emotionally because even though we were right about our reprimand, we were wrong about how we did it. Even pure accidents happen without a violent motive. So a sincere, embarrassing apology will help heal an offended child. Remember the definition of Love in 1 Corinthians 13.

When you have to spank or punish your kids, never do it while you are angry. It's a good practice to tell them that they are in trouble and that in one hour we are going to talk about it. That gives you time to cool off and pray about what is the best thing to do. When you cool off, you can think clearly. Then, if you have to spank them, be reasonable for the infraction. Explain why you have to do this, and when you are done, hold your child, love them, and pray for them until they are better. This reinforces the consequences of doing what their actions deserve and communicates to them that you are there to help them avoid more serious consequences. Trust me, when you follow this path, you will not have to do it very many times. Your kids will know that what you do, you have to do because it is your responsibility to help them understand the consequences of their actions.

It also tells them that you feel their pain, you hurt **with** them, and you forgive them. When you mess up and cause pain to your kids, you can offer to let them spank you, too! I had to do that once. Do you know what my little girl did? She forgave me and hugged me and cried with me like I did with her when she got a spanking. So watch out for offense and deal with it wisely because if you choose that door to walk through, it's a steep path to the destruction of everything you value. It's also the easiest time to turn around and run to Father!

After allowing yourself to get offended, if you don't run to your Heavenly Father, you are also breaking your Basic Trust in Him. If you choose the door of offense, you are choosing not to trust in Your Heavenly Father, and you are simultaneously running to the father of lies— who you will obey(John 8:28). This is why the downward spiral through this progression can go so horribly fast and be so destructive.

I was introduced to the concept of Sonship by a great Father, Jack Frost. He wrote several books, but the specific one—from which I learned about the 12 steps of progression to the orphan heart—is called "From Spiritual Slavery to Spiritual Sonship". I also practically memorized his messages about this subject. He passed away in 2013, but his wife, Trisha Frost, and son, Joshua Frost, are currently doing an amazing job continuing his legacy. Go to Shilohplace.org and check out the materials they have.

Warning Sign #2–A Wounded Heart

If we choose offense, it wounds our heart. Then the reasoning comes. We begin to think and feel like we have the right to be offended and bitter. As bitterness takes root, we become overwhelmed by the feeling of rejection, grief, and disappointment. Sometimes we don't recognize offense because it came for a very good reason, but we will recognize feelings of rejection, grief, and disappointment. If you recognize these signs in your heart, make the choice right now to turn and run to your Heavenly Father. If you don't, you will eventually feel like God has rejected you, left you, and forgotten about you. This is what happened to Gideon in Judges 6.

"Pardon me, my Lord," Gideon replied, "but if the Lord is with us, why has all this happened to us? Where are all his wonders that our ancestors told us about when they said, 'Did not the Lord bring us up

out of Egypt?' But now the Lord has abandoned us and given us into the hand of Midian."
(Judges 6:13 NIV)

The Israelites had turned from God to follow their own ways. Because of this, they were taken prisoner by their enemy. Gideon felt like God had left and forgotten them. But it wasn't true! Father wasn't the one who left. They were! All they had to do was turn back to Him in their heart. That's what Gideon did, and Father rescued them! But if we don't turn back to Our Father, things will get worse.

Warning Sign #3–Now Basic Trust is gone.

We didn't lose it. We gave it away to follow our new father, the father of lies (John 8:29-29). Like Esau, at this point, we have given up our inheritance, our heart of Sonship, and our connection to Father. We have traded in the heart of a Son for the broken, orphaned heart that feels completely abandoned.

When my girls were babies, they had full faith and trust in me and their mother. Eventually, that trust was violated. For my oldest daughter, it was when I put eye drops in her eyes. When she was about 1, she was tired and in need of a nap, and like all of us, she was rubbing her eyes. I was a new dad with my first kid. I was thinking, "Put in some eye drops, she'll feel better, and I'll be her hero!" But it didn't happen that way! When that first drop hit her eye, she screamed and cried like I just poked her eye out. It didn't hurt her, but it did scare her. I had no idea that was going to happen! From that day until she turned 20, she had a very difficult time putting drops in her eyes. Ironically, she started working for an optometrist and now she puts drops in the eyes of patients all day!

Children have a desire to trust and believe in everyone. This is why it is so easy to lie, fool, and take advantage of a child. They want to trust us! We are born with this Basic Trust. But eventually something happens. Whether by accident or on purpose, physically, mentally, spiritually, emotionally, or financially, someone does or doesn't do what we expected, and we get hurt. We become disappointed and emotionally injured. It happens in every relationship. Basic Trust is lost, and we have to make a choice to run away **from** or run **to** our Father.

Forgiveness alone does not restore basic trust. It's a first step, but only a change of heart will restore basic trust. We must choose to give up our pride, let Father restore our Basic Trust, and make room for healing in our hearts. If not, we will run and hide with our bleeding hearts, leaving a trail of blood for the enemy to find us. I know I just rubbed salt in an open wound. But please hear me out. Healing is available if we choose to take it!

Basic Trust is different from regular trust. Here's an example. One time, I was changing a light switch in this lady's house. She was pretty smart, and I know she knew her breakers pretty well. When I went to change the switch, she asked if I wanted her to turn off the breaker. Since I know the rules of electricity, I will sometimes make these changes without turning off the power; I just have to be more careful. Also, I wear rubber-coated gloves because I'm clumsy.

She turned off the breaker, and I began working on the switch. Usually, even if I turn off the breaker, I will double-check the power with my tester to make sure there is no power. Sometimes I will also touch the neutral wire to the hot wire on purpose to test it before I really start working. Why? If the power is still on, I don't want to be surprised! I have been shocked too many times not to do that!

So I have lost basic trust in people, tools, and even myself when it comes to electricity because I've been zapped too many times! In this case, she turned off the wrong breaker, and I didn't test it with the tester. Which was a very dumb thing for me to do! So when I touched the ground wire to the hot wire, accidentally, BOOM! Lightning flashed! I yelled! She screamed and ran out of the room yelling at me, "Are you still alive?" Needless to say, we found the correct breaker!

After that, basic trust in anyone to turn off the power was lost. Will I trust her or anyone else to turn off the breaker next time and not test the circuit to verify that the power is off? No. Would I trust her to tell me the truth about something other than breaker switches? Yes. Or do I still believe in her character? Absolutely. Do I still believe she is honest and trustworthy? Yes. So trust is still there, but I've lost basic trust in humanity to turn off the correct breaker, and with good reason! In this example, it's probably a good thing this happened. Hopefully, I have learned my lesson and will at least test to see if there is still power before I start working on anything. Actually, this is standard practice for electricians. Also, we will even disconnect the power so it cannot even be accidentally turned on while we are working on it. A lesson learned that I will never forget.

So the issue with Basic trust is not inherently bad. It's actually good. If we get hurt by something, we hopefully never forget and never do it again. It is very effective. And it is just as helpful when it comes to people. If someone hurts you, you know not to trust them in that way ever again until they can prove themselves and earn that trust back. This is the protective element of life designed by Our Heavenly Father to protect us from predators, danger, and our enemy. It creates common sense, although common sense is actually a secondary purpose. The primary purpose of this violation is to be a warning signal with one instruction:

RUN BACK TO FATHER IMMEDIATELY!

This is how Basic Trust is restored. The truth is that if you follow that process all the way to the end, the result is disaster! What I am trying to say is that in every situation where people are involved and we encounter pain, if we simply cut them off, we will end up alone and depressed.

Building boundaries with people is important.

We can only trust our Heavenly Father for everything. In my situation with the light switch, in my heart, I ran to my Father asking what to do and how to handle this situation. Immediately, He comforted me and I heard Him say, "You know better. Don't blame this on her." So when she came back apologizing, I didn't get mad and yell at her for almost killing me. I swallowed my pride and calmed **her** down, telling **her** that it was **my fault.** I am the electrician here, and I know better. I am responsible for my own choices.

Was it really my fault? No. She was confident that she had the right breaker and insisted that I believe that she knew what she was doing. This was an opportunity for our relationship to be destroyed, but with My Father's help, it was not only saved but strengthened!

You can use this with your wife too! It's absolutely required when you are wrong, but when you are right, and she gets offended by something you did, stop and run to Father. Do what He says and see what happens! This one action performed, seemingly a million times, saved my marriage. Eventually, and surprisingly, sooner than I thought, she started apologizing when I knew I was in the wrong. Your Heavenly Father knows what He is doing. He is not the problem, we are!

When we do not run back to Father for comfort, healing, and instruction, the orphan sneaks in undetected and births offense. Just like electricity, or any other power or force, we must manage the use and follow the rules.

We have been given two rules of life to follow:

1) Eat from the Tree of Life!
2) Do NOT eat from the Tree of the Knowledge of Good and Evil without God!

Our Heavenly Father is our Tree of Life! We should run to Him for every occasion, good or bad. (Matthew 13:3) When we run back to Him and absorb His Life, healing and wisdom come. We gain confidence in Him and know what to do. When the pain of our injury is healed, God's love within us makes room for compassion and we do not get offended; we have a desire to administer His healing to the one who hurt or disappointed us. This is how Sons of God live. The rain falls on the righteous and the unrighteous.

…that you may be children of your Father in heaven. He causes his sun to rise on the evil and the good, and sends rain on the righteous and the unrighteous. (Matthew 5:45 NIV).

Bad things happen to everyone because we live in a dark, ugly, selfish, destructive world. So our objective is not to change the world.

Our objective is to make the right choices so we can be light to the people in the world and healing to the broken-hearted.

If we can just do that, the choice for them to run to our Heavenly Father is clear. And if they don't, well, they've made their choice.

Do you see where this is going? Life is not all about "me". Life from my perspective is about **YOU**! My concern is not about what **I** look like for **my** benefit. My concern is what **I** look like for **YOUR** benefit!

Our enemy's first priority is to twist that up and get us to focus on our pain, our hurt, our feelings, our image, our wants, our desires, and our needs.

Jesus broke the curse of sin and death by **NOT** thinking about **His** pain and embarrassment on the cross. But while enduring His pain, He was thinking about **our** pain and how with this one event, He would make room now for healing to come into our hearts. He would eventually wipe away every tear and give us glorified bodies! This is the Message of the Gospel! This is how we are to take up our cross and follow after Him as He commanded! In all the pain that we have experienced, Jesus never left us! He was right there suffering **with** us, making Himself available to us and hoping that we would turn to Him for comfort and healing because He already took it all!

Warning Sign #4–Gentle guidance is replaced by rules.

At this point, our relationship with God begins to become a set of religious rules. We believe in the false hope that if we can simply be given or make a rule to follow, maybe, hopefully, we can earn God's approval. Our Father, whom we once received love and tender words from, has been traded out for a liar. Our new father, the father of lies, is rigid, controlling, and unmerciful.

A desperate desire to do what is right without having to apologize and reconcile relationships arises from the pain of the now orphaned heart. In this phase we will not be able to receive praise or corrections from anyone. We'll want to ask, in desperation, what we need to do to please those we interact with. If we find ourselves asking this question, we for sure know that we are thinking from the attitude of an orphaned heart. Our motivation is no longer to reconcile relationships but to seek vindication and revenge to prove that we were right all along! We want the peace we once knew to return, but not at our expense.

If you relate to these circumstances, you know that your heart has been damaged to this degree of the orphaned heart. Stop and return! You have a loving Father waiting, and He can redeem you! If we don't, we'll sink deeper into emotional pain, and since relationships are not working anymore, we will close our hearts to others.

Warning Sign #5–We close our hearts and become defensive.

Because we refuse to change our hearts and reconcile relationships by turning to Father for help, we become very defensive of our reasoning and begin to withdraw from everyone. Emotionally and spiritually at first, then physically as well. It will start with one person whom we ran away from because we were offended, then another, and another until there is no one left. Then we change jobs, change churches, end our marriage, and run away only to create the same problems all over again. With each offense, we close our hearts more and more and avoid confrontation of any kind. Conversation with God becomes very one-sided. We will always be complaining and rarely listening to Him. Then we write off hearing from God and conclude that it's not possible, even though at one time it was normal. Conversations with our wives and friends will become dry and very surface-level. Sex is not an act of love anymore but a means to fulfill a need. At church, we act like everything is ok, but it's not, and we avoid several people because they are so irritating. We might talk with some if we feel like we are better than they are or if they have something we need. We will avoid getting to know someone new unless it helps us get something we want. We will feel alone and unable to share our feelings of fear or love because our "Love tank" is empty. The definition of love changes from 1 Corinthians 13 love to lust. If you feel like this in any area of your life, stop and turn around. Your Father loves you and is still there.

Warning Sign #6–We move from a healthy dependence on others to an unhealthy independence.

Now that we have cut ourselves off from others emotionally and God spiritually, we conclude that no one will help us, and we will have to do everything ourselves. And our attitude is so bad that no one can do anything good enough to satisfy our standards or our approval. We will hear ourselves say, "Well, if nobody will help me, I'll just do it myself!" This is common and even praised in the world. There is a healthy attitude of independence from people, but this comes from the desire to trust in Our Father instead of trusting in people. I guarantee that if we determine to depend only on Father, He will quickly and wisely show us how to work with other people and depend on them because we trusted in our Father **first**.

Warning Sign #7–We need to be in control either passively or actively.

After being hurt by people we trusted time and time again, without trusting in Father, we find ourselves needing to control people, especially those we feel are weaker than we are, like women and children. In the beginning stages of this progression—in which we can live like a functioning alcoholic while controlling those weaker than us—we are afraid of those who are stronger. These are equal signs of the depth of the orphaned heart. This is very common and sneaks up on us before we realize it's a problem. It's a warning signal to stop, turn around, repent, and apologize to the one you are attempting to control. When we feel like everything is out of control because we were not in control in the first place, we need to back off, determine in our heart that we need a change, and run to our Father for help. If we do not turn around, we become afraid of people. We will bully around the weaker ones, trying to act tough, but it's just a fake front because inside, we are really scared.

Warning Sign #8–Relationships suddenly become superficial.

Since we are afraid of people, even though we are in complete denial of it, and we discover that we must have contact with others to survive, all our conversations become very superficial. If we're not controlling someone weaker, we are overly flattering someone we feel is greater than we are in order to gain something.

At this stage, we are unable to open up to anyone, so we start acting like we think others want us to act. We believe that we have fooled everyone and successfully camouflaged all our faults. The truth is that almost everyone knows there is something wrong, they just might not be able to pinpoint what it is. Many will feel very uncomfortable around you, but act like everything is ok.

A "father" or "mother" will pick up on the issues and may approach us to help, but we will lie and cover up the issue. Then they know we have a problem and cannot be trusted. This is when, even though we are the most qualified or experienced with a certain job or function, we get relieved of our duties. We just can't be trusted anymore. And eventually ,most everyone is afraid to interact with us because we are so unstable and controversial.

Worse than all of this, we cannot see how bad off we are. It's weird how we can feel so much pain and do nothing but focus on our pain while at the same time we can't see how bad it really is and who we are infecting. I have been at this point so many times. I felt so sad and frustrated, but also very entitled to feel that way. I had so deeply convinced myself that I deserved to feel sad and mad that I could not see how I was affecting other people. I couldn't receive correction or affirmation, so my wife and kids would never confront me or help me with my issues.

This causes serious emotional issues at home. Communication is extremely limited to outbursts of anger, sadness, and reclusion. As a dad, I can see when our kids shrink back and refuse to talk with us freely. Then when we know that healing needs to come, it may be **our** heart that needs it the most.

Warning Sign #9–Depression hits.
Because of the coldness we have shown to everyone around us, our orphaned heart will believe the lie that no one can or will ever help us. Depression begins as we struggle to follow all the rules and fail. Depression is also caused by the constant introspective searching for solutions without finding any. At this stage, sometimes a person can still function but be very limited. A serious turnaround is needed, and help is always available.

Warning Sign #10–Now we have no safe place to rest.
At this point, rest is almost impossible. Sleep is either difficult or all we want to do is sleep. The turmoil in our heart and mind is nerve-racking.

We can't rest at home because we have hurt and distanced ourselves from our wives and kids. They are increasingly afraid of us and are hurt and offended, too. They will act like everything is ok, but close their hearts to us and pull away. They are beginning their own path of orphaning their heart because of our actions. Even here, we can do something about it! If we don't do it for ourselves, we need to do it for our wives and kids.

Warning Sign #11–Addictions take root.
Because we were created by a Loving Father to love others and be loved, we will look for a replacement and comfort for the agonizing pain. We will begin to seek out anything that brings us pleasure.

Everything that we try will taste sweet but end with bitterness. But it's our only relief. So we'll return to it, and before long, it will become a habit. We can begin to hunger for and relish in the **power** over others and take all the glory for ourselves. We could begin to seek **possessions** to relieve the pain. Having things is not bad, but sacrificing your family, your health and your relationship with Father only to make some more money (or buy one more thing so you can be happy like the other guy) is not healthy. Anything can become a distraction and a deadly blow at this point. Everyone knows about drug, alcohol, and sex abuse, which are common and deadly addictions we use to cover or numb our pain.

Not so obvious addictions can be disguised as anything, such as watching television, eating, working, sports, shopping and social media. Anything that keeps us from spending quality time with our Father and our family can easily become an addiction, as it is replacing the love we should be receiving from God.

And get ready, if we continue playing with the addictions, thinking we have control, we are dangerously close to it controlling us. Our enemy has us in his sights to destroy us and everything around us in just a matter of time.

I thank our Father in Heaven that it is never too late to turn to Him! Sometimes we have decided to let things go too far, so if we can see that we are out of control, it's not too late.

Warning Sign #12–What you thought you were controlling is controlling you.

That is the next and last step! In this last phase, we are being controlled by our addictions, and the immense pain of our orphaned heart controls everything we do. It has become a spiritual problem. Evil spirits control destructive habits and take over because we gave them all our authority to do so. We find ourselves being dragged through life uncontrollably because we are, and we feel like there is no way out.

At this stage, we could be anybody with any social or financial status. We could be the guy begging for money on the street corner, a famous actor, a successful businessman or a pastor of a successful church. A person with a position and success is absolutely not immune to offense, resulting in a totally spiritually orphaned heart headed to complete destruction. This is why we should never judge and condemn others! We are all vulnerable to the same sneaky offenses. At this point, the orphan feels completely lost and defeated because he is.

Right now, we need a real Father, and we can't find one because we have been so distant from everyone and exchanged the Good One for a bad one. What we must do is turn to Our Heavenly Father, no matter where we are in the progression. He can and will deliver us. Maybe we have hurt everyone around us. We will have to begin to repair those relationships with wisdom and guidance from Father and some earthly fathers of ours.

The next steps.

When we repent and return to Father, we should keep our revelation to ourselves until we really get a grip on things. We need to let everyone see the results, then when they ask, we can tell them what has changed so far. We shouldn't go running around telling everyone that we have changed. This is the voice of the orphan heart again! He is trying to trap us into pleasing others only to gain their trust. After recovery, it's pretty easy to slip back into orphan thinking because it became a way of life, and now we are living a new way of life. Simply start attempting to do things right. It will take time, there may be some falls to temptation and plenty of failures, but keep going! Start thinking of others' feelings as more valuable than your own. Tackle and master one issue at a time. Don't try to stop doing all the things that people and religion say are "bad". You'll just be trying to follow the rules to earn the right standing with everyone again. Get on a Bible reading program. Get in a group and establish some accountability with a mentor. Take it one day at a time.

Now obviously, if what you are doing is harmful to others, immoral, or illegal, quit it now! If you need help, throw your pride out the door and go get help.

If we really turn, change fathers, and seek our Heavenly Father's perfect will to be done in our lives, we will want to do whatever it takes to put a stop to all our unhealthy habits. We may have had great, bad, or even non-existent parents. In any case, we will have the tendency to act like the father/mother we had because that's all we know. Our earthly father acted like he did because his father acted like he did. So we shouldn't blame our dads or our moms for our problems. Just overcome them.

Take ownership of this revelation and:

Become a father to someone in need.

This is how we will find fathers in the land: we become fathers! If we hunger for a father in our lives and can't find one, we need to be a father. We start by being a better husband. Don't tell anyone. Just do it. We start by being a better father to our kids. Don't tell them what's going on; they'll see and eventually ask when we have painstakingly proven our integrity and our love for them. We need to love our wives like never before, despite their faults. Our kids see and respect the love we show towards our wives. We need to find things we love about her and cast all the other stuff on our Father. He will change her if He needs to.

We don't have to be right anymore.

Apologize and genuinely ask for forgiveness even if you think you are right. Honor your wife and kids. Let them be right, as long as they aren't hurting themselves, and sacrifice your wants and desires for theirs. If we've been acting out of an orphaned heart, we have a lot to prove and a lot to make up for, so let it take its course. It may take years ,and it may not. We don't care how long it takes as long as we have the right Father!

Friend, I have some good news! You are not ever so bad off that Father can't rescue you! I know you can't see how, but if you're just willing to be willing to give Him a chance, He can be, once again, your Father because He is your Redeemer. You can't do it on your own. He is the only one who can change you because He's the only one who lives in your pain with you and is thinking of your pain instead of His own. He's the only one who bled for you and died for you and raised Himself up so He could redeem you!

Questions

What was something cool about building the shed that you learned today?

_____

_____

When and where will you spend 5 minutes with God today?

_____

_____

What belief about yourself has changed today?

_____

_____

How can you be a better dad, a better husband, or a better friend/mentor?

_____

_____

CHAPTER EIGHT

Go and Do!
The Age of the Doers

Let's Paint some Shed!

Almost everyone knows how to put some paint on a wall and call it good, and most of the time that's all it takes. But actually, after we've spent all the time and money to build our shed, in just a few short years, it will be irreparable from water damage, sunshine, heat, and ice if we do not put on the right paint and maintain it with fresh paint every few years.

There are many kinds of paint that are used for many different uses. Paint on interior walls is not just pretty ,but it also protects the walls from damage and promotes cleanliness. The better quality paints actually have some mold-resistant chemicals included, which is nice to have in the case of water contact. We will be using an exterior paint to seal off the wood and help protect it from moisture rot. Exterior paints are of higher quality and a little more expensive because they have UV light inhibitors in them, and some have mold-resistant chemicals.

Most of the time, your project will require two coats. The wood we used is water-resistant and has a primer paint already on it. I like to start painting the main body with two coats, and then if the trim is a different color, paint the trim with two coats. I use 9" roller pads with a ¾" nap for the walls, and for the trim, I'll use a 4" mini roller.

Just like painting, in this session we will cover a few subjects which will help wrap up this project and send us out into Life a new Man, a Man Under Construction!

The Age of the Doers

"When he saw the crowds, he had compassion on them because they were confused and helpless, like sheep without a shepherd. He said to his disciples, "The harvest is great, but the workers are few. So pray to the Lord who is in charge of the harvest; ask him to send more workers into his fields." (Matthew 9:36-38 NLT).

I always thought this meant that we need more preachers, and that is partially true. Now, I think it actually means that there is plenty of work out there to do—many people are lost and need to hear the Good News. But pastors and preachers cannot do it all. Actually, they are not supposed to be the ones going out to reach the lost. They are supposed to train up, equip, and build up the church so we can go out and win the lost like dads trying to find their lost children.

"Now these are the gifts Christ gave to the church: the apostles, the prophets, the evangelists, and the pastors and teachers. Their responsibility is to equip God's people to do his work and build up the church, the body of Christ." (Ephesians 4:11-12 NLT).

We are the ones who are supposed to be winning the lost! Where? At church! At home! At our job! At the grocery store! Everywhere we go! Our feet are covered with Readiness, and our hearts so full of love and forgiveness that we can share what we have with the next person we meet. We should all be "fisherman" and "Light to the world" all day, every day, everywhere we go.

To me, people in the world are like little blueberries or strawberries. They must be hand-picked, and because great care is required, only the Family can do that job. This is OUR JOB. Not the pastor's job.

"So you see, faith by itself isn't enough. Unless it produces good deeds, it is dead and useless. Now, someone may argue, "Some people have faith; others have good deeds." But I say, "How can you show me your faith if you don't have good deeds? I will show you my faith by my good deeds." (James 2:17-18 NLT).

We are in the age of the Doers!

Go and Do Likewise.

Jesus replied with a story: "A Jewish man was traveling from Jerusalem down to Jericho, and he was attacked by bandits. They stripped him of his clothes, beat him up, and left him half dead beside the road. "By chance, a priest came along. But when he saw the man lying there, he crossed to the other side of the road and passed him by. A Temple assistant walked over and looked at him lying there, but he also passed by on the other side. "Then a despised Samaritan came along, and when he saw the man, he felt compassion for him. Going over to him, the Samaritan soothed his wounds with olive oil and wine and bandaged them. Then he put the man on his own donkey and took him to an inn, where he took care of him. The next day he handed the innkeeper two silver coins, telling him, 'Take care of this man. If his bill runs higher than this, I'll pay you the next time I'm here.' "Now, which of these three would you say was a neighbor to the man who was attacked by bandits?" Jesus asked. The man replied, "The one who showed him mercy." Then Jesus said, "Yes, now go and do the same." (Luke 10:30-37 NLT).

This is "Doing"! We cannot be too clean to help someone dirty or too important to help someone in need. We need to have plenty of Love, forgiveness, finances, time, wisdom, and emotional stability in reserve to share when the time comes. This is more impossible, yet easier than it sounds! More impossible because only Father can empower us to constantly be ready to help others, and easier because it is Our Father who will help us when He calls.

Communication

Relationships are created from open and honest conversation. Quality conversation is an art that requires much intentional effort. Recently, I asked My Father to teach me how to have meaningful and productive conversations with people when the circumstances arise. I found my conversation draining the patience of my listener, and I didn't understand why. I wanted to be life-giving, not life-taking.

Then one morning, I was talking with a guy at church. He was telling me about all his problems at home. Problems with his kids, his job, his family, and eventually, problems with people at the church. I listened carefully to what he had to say until he started kind of repeating himself. I thought he would eventually ask me what I thought about his situation, but he just kept talking, talking, talking ,and talking. I was getting so tired of listening to him! Finally, I told him that I had to go and he said goodbye and we parted. Then I ran into one of our pastors, and I started talking about my life with him. Next thing I knew, I was doing the same thing to our beloved pastor. I was so upset with myself! What I despised, I was doing and didn't even see it! I ended that conversation when I realized what I had done. So I marched out to my truck and drove off, asking what I was doing wrong. Then, just like that, Father began to educate me.

He reminded me that it is the orphan spirit that steals life from others. The orphan spirit is starving for love, so it will steal love and attention from others any time it has the opportunity. Our "plate" must be full or we will steal from others with our conversation.

When we are talking with someone and we ask them a question, we are actually taking emotional and spiritual food from their plate and putting it on our plate. In that case, at first, they are offering the food from their plate, which is ok. But when we talk too long about our issues and complain, argue or gossip, we actually begin to steal food off of the listener's plate. They will listen for a little while out of kindness, but when they start to feel drained—because the food on their plate is disappearing quickly—they become increasingly uncomfortable and will eventually make an excuse and leave.

This is also why some people are very introverted and don't want to start a conversation with someone. They are afraid of losing the little emotional food they have. Sometimes we talk with someone because we want their attention, affirmation, or gratitude. We brag about our life, talking about all the great things we or our kids have done. Inside, we are thinking, "They gave us this food before, so hopefully they will do it again! If not, I'll ask a question or tell a story in hopes of starting some kind of transfer of food from their plate to mine again."

Sometimes we are willingly administering information like when a teacher, coach, pastor, or leader is giving instructions. We are willingly handing out food from our plate to the listener. Also, if in conversation we ask how the listener is doing or how something is in their life, we are taking food from our plate and putting it on theirs. When we are telling our story, with the intention to bless someone, we begin dispensing food to our listeners' plates. But if we take too long or it's not a blessing to them anymore, we actually begin stealing food from their plate again.

People want to hear what you have to say because you are FEEDING them! People don't want to listen to what you have to say if you are STEALING from them.

In a healthy conversation, both parties are offering the food on their plates to each other. Orphans cannot offer their emotional food on their plate to another person because they feel like they don't have enough. Orphans must steal off everyone else's plate because they will not eat off their own plate because they're so afraid they are going to run out of food and starve.

A Son has total and complete confidence that his plate will be constantly refilled by his Heavenly Father with never-ending amounts of emotional food. This is true in every area of life. We cannot give what we do not have! We will be tight with our giving if we think that may be all we get. We will be joyfully generous if we know that the supply is constant, never late, and never ending. We give because we have.

What do you have? Father is not concerned about how much we have. He is most interested in whether we will give what we do have. Remember who you are working with here! With a word, galaxies were formed.

"Then the Lord asked him, "What is that in your hand?" "A shepherd's staff," Moses replied." (Exodus 4:2 NLT).

With that simple stick, our Heavenly Father parted the Red Sea and numerous other impossible things. What can He do with what you "HAVE"?

But Jesus said, "You feed them." "With what?" they asked. "We'd have to work for months to earn enough money to buy food for all these people!" "How much bread do you have?" he asked. "Go and find out." They came back and reported, "We have five loaves of bread and two fish." (Mark 6:37-38 NLT).

With five loaves and two fish, Jesus fed 5000 men, plus women and children, which were not counted. I am guilty of not thinking I have enough to do what Father is asking me to do. The truth is that we should never think that. He will not ask for what we do not have, and He can make what we have enough. Praise The Lord. That is so awesome. Our Father is Awesome.

Walking on the Water

I was at the church during prayer time, and I felt like I should stand up and walk and pray, so I stood up and I started walking in circles in a small open area right in front of where I was sitting. I was looking down at the floor, and as I walked, I felt like I was seeing something that wasn't really there. I was having a vision. In my vision, the floor looked like water. There were little tiny waves, and I could hear and feel the splashing of the water like I was walking through a puddle. I noticed that my shoes were getting wet. I just kept walking around, all amazed and super excited that I was finally walking on water. This is something I always wanted to do.

The Sea of Uncertainty

Then, as I was looking at the water, it suddenly got really deep! So it wasn't like the floor was just wet. It was like I was standing in a deep pool of water. I felt amazed and totally safe and confident that Father had empowered me to walk on something as uncertain as water. Then the Holy Spirit began to explain to me that when we trust in Him, we could be stable even on something as uncertain as water. He called it the Sea of Uncertainty. Father told me that this is how He taught Jesus to learn to trust Him. He called Jesus out onto the water to show Him that when He trusted His Father more than everything else, He could walk or live above what was uncertain.

I thought that was pretty extreme because water is very uncertain if you're going to try to stand on it. Then Father continued to explain to me that we are all living and walking on the Sea of Uncertainty, and we don't know it. The disciples thought that they could trust in their boat. Even though men normally can trust a boat, when the wind and rain come, their trusty boat might sink. It's not really so trustworthy after all. Then he explained that people feel confident and safe walking around on dry ground with solid rock under their feet. But little do they know, there is a sea of water under them, too! Then, under that is an ocean of liquid lava, and we know that either of those could erupt from the eart,h and our rock would sink immediately. The ground on which we stand is uncertain. So the Truth is that trusting in our Father for Certainty is much better than trusting in anything created. Trust in your Father and walk on the Sea of Uncertainty.

The disciples were all trusting in their boat—which was about to sink—when they saw Jesus. Then Jesus told them to come out onto the water. But Peter was the only one who could trust Jesus that much. And he walked on the water too.

This is what we are supposed to do. Walk on the Sea of Uncertainty, trusting in Father as we go, but then call someone else out with you so they can learn how to walk on water too. Teach them, by example, how to trust in your Heavenly Father with you. This is what I was doing when I showed you how to use tools and build this shed of ours! Is it perfect? Nope! Will you stay dry walking on the Sea of Uncertainty? Nope! It's not a perfect walk, but it is an amazingly "Godlike" way of living life! I think this is where the phrase, "Getting your feet wet," came from. It means that we are going to start to do something we are uncertain about. It might get a little mess,y but that's ok, our goal is not to stay dry, our goal is to stay above the water and take someone with us.

"But be doers of the word, and not hearers only, deceiving yourselves." (James 1:22 NKJV).

This is the life of The Doer! Be a Doer of the Word and Do what you believe, or you will deceive and trick yourself into believing you are someone you are not.

"But why do you call Me 'Lord, Lord,' and not do the things which I say? Whoever comes to Me, and hears My sayings and does them, I will show you whom he is like: He is like a man building a house, who dug deep and laid the foundation on the rock. And when the flood arose, the stream beat vehemently against that house, and could not shake it, for it was founded on the rock. But he who heard and did nothing is like a man who built a house on the earth without a foundation, against which the stream beat vehemently; and immediately it fell. And the ruin of that house was great." (Luke 6:46-49 NKJV).

Let's get our feet wet and be a Doer.

It's ok to get your feet wet!
A word from my Pastor, Josh Blount.

Life is uncertain and unpredictable. It's a product of tremendous creativity. Life is a beautiful barrage of colors, sounds, tastes, smells, and textures exploding into more of the same while maintaining order and purpose. And even though we would prefer creativity to be 100% predictable, it is not. That is the "God" part of **creativity**. The part that is predictably unpredictable.

We work for hours, weeks, and years thinking that we can create exactly what we envisioned. But when we are done, the finished product may be similar or it may be totally opposite of what we originally intended. Yet after what feels like failure after failure, we continue to strive to create. Actually, we will never end up with what we set out to create. Why not just quit? We don't quit because perfection is not the requirement.

**Faithfulness is the requirement,
And we were made for this!**

King Solomon said that God has set eternity in our hearts.

"Yet God has made everything beautiful for its own time. He has planted eternity in the human heart, but even so, people cannot see the whole scope of God's work from beginning to end." (Ecclesiastes 3:11 NLT).

We ache for meaning and purpose. We deeply desire to do work that matters. We long for something more than just survival. We were created to partner with God (just like Adam) in the work of cultivating and now restoring His creation in this broken world. Our work will never quite feel finished, but that's not where the story ends.

One day, in the Kingdom of Heaven, our work will be redeemed! We will create without exhaustion, build without striving, and labor without pain, working for the sheer joy of it. And when we stand before Jesus, we will finally hear the words we've been longing to hear:

It is Finished

Until then, we press on. We love our wives, our kids, our community, and show up for our church. We give, sow, and labor, not because it's easy, but because it's **good**. Even when our work feels small, frustrating, imperfect, and unfinished.

God is Using it All

One day, the work will be complete, the struggle will be over, and the toil will turn to joy. But until then, we wake up, show up and Co-Create like we were made to.

Faithfulness
I desperately want a Father in my life!

"I do not write these things to shame you, but as my beloved children, I warn you. For though you might have ten thousand instructors in Christ, yet you do not have many fathers; for in Christ Jesus I have begotten you through the gospel. Therefore, I urge you, imitate me. For this reason, I have sent Timothy to you, who is my beloved and faithful son in the Lord, who will remind you of my ways in Christ, as I teach everywhere in every church." (I Corinthians 4:14-17 NKJV).

After everything we have learned, I am drawn to one conclusion: I need a Father in my life! Paul was made aware of this deep need in the lives of men and women of his day. And the "day" is the same. When we realize that we have been poor sons and made plenty of mistakes, we long for a good father to help us, but we usually don't find one. What do we do then?

BE A FATHER!
We all need to follow our Heavenly Father as Jesus followed His Heavenly Father. But we also need to BE the example of a good Son who follows his Father. So be a faithful Son of God, but when a lost Son crosses your path, be a good Father to him. Be an example of Grace, Mercy, Wisdom, Strength with Gentleness, Peac,e and Provision to this little one who needs a dad. Show the one with an orphaned heart that they are loved just like they are, and therefore

they don't have to be broken anymore! They don't have to be slaves or prisoners anymore. They can be free as they follow you, following Your Heavenly Father, walking on the Sea of Uncertainty, feeding them as you go.

The Final Word

You are not alone. I have been through all of this and am still going through it every day. The Sea of Uncertainty is just as uncertain for me as it is for everyone else. Life was not meant to be lived alone, so don't do it.

As we finish up this adventure today, I leave you with these thoughts:

Be a good Son first, and then be a good Father to everyone you meet.

Love your kids. Love the good and the bad in them. Maybe the bad is a strong character that will make them GREAT later in life!

Love your wife as you love yourself. Honor her as the stronger person. She is your helper in life, your co-creator, your partner, and friend who you will grow old and grey with.

Don't do life alone.

Turn to Your Heavenly Father for everything.

Strive to become the best Son you can possibly be. Watch out for that orphan! He is only out to destroy you. Resist him and replace orphan attitudes and habits with Son attitudes and Son habits.

Stay in the Word.

Spend 5 minutes a day with Him.

Pray the Father's prayer faithfully. Remember, it's not for Him, it's for you!

And finally, enjoy the day. Smell the flowers, hug your kids, kiss your wife, and be a good friend for no reason at all, except because that's who you are.

You are a son of God, a Man Under Construction!

Questions:

What is one thing you learned from the last 2 months that you want to incorporate or have incorporated into your life?

_____

_____

How would you like to continue from here? What would you like to do next?

_____

_____

What aspects about this project did you like?

_____

_____

What aspects about this project did you not like?

_____

_____

What about this project would you like to change or add?

_____

_____

What questions do you have?

_____

_____

What subjects would you like to understand more?

_____

_____

ABOUT THE AUTHOR

Joel Brentlinger is an entrepreneur, mentor, and ministry leader whose life's work bridges business and faith. With decades of experience spanning ranching, business management, restaurants, remodeling, and construction, Joel has built a reputation for resilience and leadership across multiple industries. Beyond his professional accomplishments, he has devoted more than 30 years to serving children and families through his local church, where his influence has shaped generations.

A proud father, grandfather, and spiritual father to many, Joel now channels his experience and calling into a mission to restore the hearts of children to their fathers and fathers to their children. His unique blend of entrepreneurial insight, pastoral care, and personal devotion makes his voice both practical and deeply inspiring for readers seeking transformation in family, faith, and purpose.

MORE BOOKS FROM Joel Brentlinger

HIS...

and HERS...

Redeeming Eve
Now Available!

Restoring God's Original Design for His Daughters
From the very start, Eve was underestimated, and Adam's silence in the garden established humanity's first error—her unrecognized glory.

The pages of this book call to every woman who wants to believe there is more inside her than the world has told her she could be. It's a declaration that you were never an afterthought, but phase 2 of Father's original, perfect design.

You'll find healing from Truth, strength from Destiny, and receive a deeper revelation of the *Eve* which God can redeem inside you.

It's time for You to be all who God created you to be.

It's time to *Redeem Eve!*

Book Joel for Speaking Engagements, Leadership Training, or Life Coaching

Contact Joel Brentlinger at:
JoelBrentlinger@gmail.com
JoelBrentlinger.org

For bulk orders contact: Bush Publishing
support@BushPublishing.com | 918-260-2883

www.ingramcontent.com/pod-product-compliance
Lightning Source LLC
Chambersburg PA
CBHW070139080526
44586CB00015B/1763